A HOUSE OF MY OWN

Family members, residents of Dulanto, stand in front of the wall for their new home. The planks in the background are a section of the wall of their old house.

A HOUSE OF MY OWN

*Social Organization
in the Squatter
Settlements of
Lima, Peru*

Susan Lobo

*With a New Preface and Conclusion
by the Author*

UNIVERSITY OF ARIZONA PRESS

Tucson & London

About the Author

Susan Lobo has carried out research in Peru since 1964. She holds a Ph.D. in anthropology from the University of Arizona. She has worked with the Ahashemem Indians in California, the Pimas in Arizona, and the Pima Bajo in Mexico. She has taught at the University of California at Berkeley and at Davis, and she was the program coordinator for the Center for Latin American Studies at Berkeley from 1981 to 1984. She has served as the research coordinator for the Community History Project at Intertribal Friendship House in Oakland since 1978 and has worked in development projects for numerous tribes and American Indian organizations throughout the United States.

Fifth printing 1992

THE UNIVERSITY OF ARIZONA PRESS

Copyright © 1982
The Arizona Board of Regents
All Rights Reserved

This book was set in 10/12 Palatino on Linotype.
Manufactured in the U.S.A.

Library of Congress Cataloging-in-Publication Data
Lobo, Susan.
    A house of my own.
    Bibliography: p.
    Includes index.
    1. Squatter settlements — Peru — Lima.   2. Lima
(Peru) — Social conditions.   3. Community development, Urban — Peru — Lima.   I. Title.
HN344.L6   307.7′6   81-16275

ISBN 0-8165-0739-2   AACR2
ISBN 0-8165-0761-9 (pbk.)

To my mother

CONTENTS

ILLUSTRATIONS

Photographs

Figures

Photo Credits and Permissions

Susan Lobo was primary photographer for *A House of My Own.*
Permission for use of additional photographs was obtained from
Frank Lobo, whose pictures are found on pages 25, 68, 109, 113,
123, and 129, and from Angela Horna de Arriaga, who supplied the
photograph on page 105.

When she photographed various settings, situations, and cere-
monial events in the squatter settlements of Dulanto and Ciudadela
Chalaca in Lima, Peru, Susan Lobo obtained permission from the
individuals involved. Most of the photographs were taken between
1964 and 1974.

PREFACE

A snow-capped mountain, two llamas on the alert, and a *cholita* dressed in clothing reminiscent of the area near Cuzco were painted on the sign above the restaurant in Jackson Heights, New York. A smaller hand-lettered sign in the window said, "Chicha," another "Picante de Cuy" (guinea pig prepared with hot sauce). "Put that in your book!" said Truyano as we walked along the street. "To show how far we all have come since you first met my family in Ciudadela Chalaca in the 1960s." He was right. Ten years after the initial publication of this book, it is appropriate to add a preface and a conclusion. This preface offers an update regarding some of the people, families, and activities described here, and the conclusion responds to the interest that readers have expressed in a fuller analytical statement than was found in the original publication.

During the ten years that have intervened since this book was first published, much has happened that has dramatically affected the people of Ciudadela Chalaca and Dulanto whose lives are described here. The deep social revolution in Peru, whose roots found expression from the 1950s to the 1970s principally in the surge of migration by highlanders from rural areas into the cities, is now expressing itself in armed confrontation. While this violence is now the most visible expression of change, a number of preceding factors have affected the process of urbanization in Lima and have had a dramatic impact on the lives of all the individuals represented here. This book was intended to focus almost exclusively on the lives of people, principally people of Quechua descent, rather than to tie that discussion to the larger national or international social context. Yet these larger social forces always created both pressures and options for change, and they continue to do so.

I conducted the research for this book during a time of hopeful dreams, visions of a better life for "our children," to be achieved through hard work and careful planning. A common refrain heard in the barriadas of Lima during that time was, "At least there is hope in the cities." In Ciudadela Chalaca and Dulanto, this hope has increasingly been shadowed during the past ten years by desperation in the face of a series of linked factors: an international debt that has produced soaring inflation and increased poverty in many sectors, an active international market in cocaine, escalating violence, and an increased migration to the coastal cities by people, often widows and orphans, who are escaping the violence of the highlands.

One of the responses to these pressures by people living in Ciudadela Chalaca and Dulanto has been to find a way to emigrate to other South American countries or to the United States. For some extended families, this migrational movement has become yet another phase in the step migration that began two or three generations before when a kinsman or woman moved from a small rural community to a highland town or city and from there to Lima.

What has become of some of the families whose lives are described here as a result of this process, and what possible implications are there for our understanding of the extension of those characteristics and conditions that inform the concept of positive adaptation? Since carrying out the initial research for this book, I have made two more relatively short field trips to Peru and have maintained contact, through letters and telephone conversations, with a network of family members of those people that I originally knew in Ciudadela Chalaca and Dulanto. Within the past five years, the increasing migration to the United States, often by individuals I knew in Peru or their kinsmen, has made it possible for me to visit and interview people living in Jackson Heights, New York; Patterson, New Jersey; Los Angeles; and the San Francisco Bay area. Many of these same people have visited me in return. The following paragraphs offer glimpses of what has happened to some of them.

Celsa is a woman of Quechua descent whose family was tied for generations as tenant laborers to a remote highland hacienda in Apurimac, where she was born. Spanish is her second language, and she speaks it with a heavy Quechua accent. She has two years of formal education. Twenty-five years ago, Celsa, seated in her very modest home in Ciudadela Chalaca, gently stroked her little daughter's hair and said, "Maybe someday my girl will visit you in the United States." I now have to admit that she had more faith in her potential than I did. At that time I remember hoping, as I looked at her ragged and patched clothes, that she and her family could make it through the week.

Her daughter has now lived for the past seven years in New York, is married, and is the mother of two children. Two of her brothers and their spouses and children live nearby. This set of siblings and their spouses knew one another throughout their childhood in Ciudadela Chalaca. They continue to maintain close contact with Peru through the coming and going of people from the area and through packages they send to their extended family there. This is a pattern of migration, reciprocity, and alliance building reminiscent of the relationship that exists between the people living in the highlands of Peru and those who have migrated to the coastal urban areas.

Celsa's daughter and her kin living in New York work in restaurants as cooks or cleaning people. To earn additional money, they work overtime as often as possible and maintain other sources of income. These practices are similar to the economic strategies their parents practiced in Peru. Celsa's daughter attended night school, obtained a nursing degree, and then gained certification as a registered nurse. With the additional earnings she will make, she and her husband plan to open their own restaurant eventually. Her children have brought Celsa to New York to care for her grandchildren.

After her first year in the United States, Celsa's relatives pooled their funds and flew her and one of her daughters-in-law to California to see the sights and to visit an anthropologist friend, myself. Years before, she and I had made the long overland journey to visit the highland hacienda where she was born. Now we laughed together, acknowledging how the world we both knew had changed within the past twenty-five years and how our mutual roles of researcher and informant had shifted, the distinction and gulf becoming blurred as our personal histories had to some extent become shared.

The history of Celsa and her family contains elements that are typical of many residents of Ciudadela Chalaca and Dulanto. Mario, who on page 52 sits reading a comic book while having his hair cut in Dulanto, is in his mid-twenties and, after stowing away on a boat from Peru, now lives in Los Angeles. He works in a restaurant "in salad preparation," and lives in a small apartment with four other *paisanos* he knew in Dulanto as a child. After living in the United States for a year and purchasing a car, he drove to Denver to visit relatives there. The oldest brother of the little girl pictured at the bottom of page 113 is Truyano who is mentioned at the beginning of this preface. Although now in his early forties, less than a year before I saw him in New York he had undertaken an arduous three-month overland journey to arrive in the United States and now lives in New York. He does janitorial work at night and studies during the day. Ava, who is quoted on page 38, has lived for the past fourteen years in Venezuela, where she owns a small knitting enterprise in partnership with three younger siblings.

Much of the pioneering optimism that characterized Ciudadela Chalaca and Dulanto twenty-five years ago is still evident in the homes of these families, and many of the same modes of positive adaptation, though transformed by time and place, continue to exist. Peruvian networks exist in Latino barrios in New York and California. Although the migrants do not build their own homes, as they did in the Peruvian squatter settlements, the creation of a "community" in many other respects is taking place. The migrants to the United States feel a strong sense of accomplishment in attaining the goals they have set for themselves, and they have a strong and positive view of themselves and of their future. Parallel to the circumstances discussed at length in the following pages, the migrants to the United States have maintained core relationships, especially strong sibling solidarity, and these relationships are once again contributing to their positive adaptation. The flexible social structure allows the migrants to use traditional methods, such as *compadrazgo*, for forming alliances to strengthen existing ties and to enter into new types of relationships. Finally, both in their words and in their actions, they enthusiastically express their self-confidence and their sense of control over their own lives. They learned all of these elements thoroughly and deeply while living in Ciudadela Chalaca and Dulanto as children.

During the past fifteen years, my research focus has shifted, though it has never entirely left the Peruvian migrants. I now work primarily with American Indian people who have migrated to the urban San Francisco Bay area from rural regions and tribal lands throughout the United States. The Native People of South America and the United States with whom I have lived and worked have patiently taught me many lessons, mainly by example. One is the need to place what is discussed in this book into a hemispheric context. The nature of what has occurred can be seen as a micro view of significant demographic shifts from rural to urban areas, and increasingly over very long distances from south to north, that have affected millions of Native People in this hemisphere. Also notable are the many parallels between the urbanization process experienced by Native People in Peru and in the United States. Whether referred to in this book or elsewhere as American Indians, campesinos, Peruvians, Quechua, or native or indigenous people, it is important to acknowledge that these are the original people of the hemisphere and that the social organization described in this book is in many respects an expression of Andean cultural forms stretching back many millennia. Forms of indigenous culture throughout the hemisphere — though often transformed, amended, or enriched — have survived demographic shifts such as those described here. There continues to exist a strong and essential cultural foundation and a tenacious cultural persistence among the first people of this hemisphere, both north and south.

ACKNOWLEDGMENTS

The following people are some of the thinkers, speakers, and dreamers who have given me the inspiration along the way to continue to appreciate and understand the ways that a Native perspective requests the attention of us all. I especially wish to thank Angela Horna de Arriaga, Domingo Arriaga, Victoria Bomberry, Jean LaMarr, Lawrence Edge, Wes Huss, Darryl Wilson, and Julian Lang. The patient understanding of my daughter, Kelina Lobo, continues ten years after the first publication of this book. I have been working on this research and the issues it raises since the day she was born, and with the help of these good friends, I expect to continue to do so for the rest of my life.

SUSAN LOBO

Oakland, California

May 1992

FOREWORD

It is difficult in the 1980s to realize how closely associated the ideas of urbanization and social disorganization once were. A view of urban life had been conceived by American anthropologists and sociologists based largely on selected aspects of cities in the United States marked by social disorganization and anomie. In 1952, however, Oscar Lewis published an article which became a landmark for American anthropologists working in urban settings. It was called "Urbanization Without Breakdown," and it served to loosen the close linkage between the concepts of urbanization and social disorganization. In the 1950s research following the lines of Lewis's work in Mexico City began to demonstrate that rural migrants arriving in the cities did not necessarily begin their adaptation to urban conditions as disorganized and disoriented individuals.

A deeper and more comprehensive understanding of the nature of city life was also emerging as less limiting theoretical frameworks began to be used in the growing number of urban investigations. The studies of Herbert Gans (1962) on "urban villagers," Elliot Liebow's (1967) revelations of life in Tally's Corner, and other discoveries of community life within the urban setting required a new formulation of the nature of urban life and a more careful examination of how it was possible for villagers to move into cities without the breakdown of rural cultural patterns and traditions of organization. By the 1970s the new ground for appreciating urbanizing processes was fairly well established, as indicated by Lisa Redfield Peattie's *The View From the Barrio* (1970) and William Mangin's collection of studies called *Peasants in Cities* (1970).

And yet, although the sophisticated few, as a result of research in Mexico, the United States, and Africa, had been able to discard old preconceptions, it was at the same time true that this hard-won knowledge did not diffuse evenly. It did not, moreover, spread among those most in need of it as they faced problems of assisting rural people of the world to adapt to the cities where everywhere they were flocking. A case in point was coastal Peru during the 1960s and 1970s. Here tens of thousands of highland villagers were moving down from the mountains to large coastal cities like Lima. There they formed what were called *barriadas*, that is, vast, closely-packed settlements of thousands which grew up suddenly in a matter of weeks and months just outside the Peruvian cities. As the barriadas multiplied, the long-time residents of Lima looked on appalled at the conditions under which the hordes of newcomers were living — not for a few months, but for year after year, as more and more migrants continued to pour in. Steadily there grew up a myth, as the author of this volume points out, concerning the nature of the inhabitants of these settlements.

It came to be generally believed that the barriadas were places of concentrated violence and sin. If, it was reasoned, the shacks and shanties in which the people lived were as substandard as they appeared to the other urban dwellers, if individuals went on living for years under conditions so terribly crowded and divergent from any imaginable human standards, then the people must be something less than human. They must be prone to constant violence and all sorts of aberrant behavior. And so, as outsiders viewed the barriadas' disordered exteriors, the myth grew that the barriada residents' behavior must be more like that of caged animals than that of normal human beings. The myth was no short-lived misunderstanding, any more than the barriadas themselves were short-lived. As late as 1978 the Peruvian anthropologist José Matos Mar asserted that, despite much attention to the barriadas on the part of urban officials and some social scientists during more than twenty years, the myth of social chaos was still all too strong an influence over those concerned with solving the problems of the new settlements.

Susan Lobo first carried out field work in 1964 in Lima and slowly became aware of a marked discrepancy between the characterization of barriada people made by city officials and social workers and the information she gleaned about them from her firsthand contacts. The idea that the migrants lived in disorder, as agglomerations of individuals without effective community life, agreed neither with her preconceptions as an anthropologist nor (and more importantly) with what she began to see about her. As she formulated a plan for living with a family in a barriada in 1974, she was warned by other Peruvians against any such foolhardy course of action. It was stressed that the people were prone to excessive violence, that they were inveterate thieves, that in short no civilized person would want to live in the barriada and that she could not expect to survive if she insisted on doing so. Dr. Lobo picked her way through what turned out to be misguided advice and promptly found that residence with a barriada family was quite feasible. She also found after what in all totaled more than a year's residence with various families that she could survive quite happily and not only survive but work at her observation and note-taking with the pleased cooperation of the families who took her in. She discovered that the situation of life in a barriada was after all a human situation to be appreciated as such. Not that it was perfectly easy to make the adjustment. On the contrary, she learned the miseries as well as the pleasures of living in a barriada community. She found that perhaps the most difficult adjustment for her, as a middle-class Anglo-American from a comfortable United States suburb, was coping with the close-packed life of these communities. This problem is brought home to the reader most vividly in her account of seeking a relatively secluded spot from the family's daily activities in order to write up some notes. No sooner was she seen to be off in a corner by herself, than the woman of the house sent one of her daughters to be with her so that she would not be all alone and therefore unhappy.

Dr. Lobo's findings, based on extended contacts and participant observation in the barriadas, are in summary that much of the highland village culture came promptly into action as the migrants organized themselves in their unaccustomed settlements. Kinship remained of vital importance, for example, but it was by no means the whole kinship system of the highlands. It was a truncated kinship system emphasizing the relations among siblings. The lineal institutions and the accompanying authority of earlier generations ceased to have application and meaning in the new setting, and the inter-sibling relationships assumed fundamental importance and became the primary cement of social life. Traditional mechanisms for alliance between kin, such as the dynamic institution of the godparent-compadrazgo system so pervasive in Latin America, were employed to knit the new communities in old ways for new purposes. New forms of association were adopted and used for fulfilling the functions which the dense settlements had to assume to meet urgent physical needs, such as waste disposal and the use of water. Thus, rather than an unorganized mass of individuals, the barriada appeared to Dr. Lobo to be a rather well-ordered community. Rather than leaving behind in the highlands their traditional forms of organization, they selected elements from the village social system which could serve the needs of the urgent adaptations required under the new conditions. Dr. Lobo describes the barriadas not as the hardly human places imagined by the viewers from the outside but rather as orderly human communities where creative adaptations take place as the needs arise. Dr. Lobo calls the processes which she observed *positive adaptation*, and there is much to be learned from her analysis.

It becomes clear from the description of life in the barriadas presented here not only that the former communities are not reconstructed item by item but that the individuals are in fundamental ways different from those, or at least most of those, who remained behind in the highlands. The migrants are a selection of people who are ready for whatever must be faced. They expect things to be different. They subscribe to a value which does not rule the lives of the highland villagers. They have come to Lima because they wish to escape what they label as *triste* in the life of the villages. Literally translated, *triste* means "sad," but what they mean is not a sadness which brings tears, but a dullness which brings boredom. The people of the barriadas have come to Lima, because, as they freely say, life is boring in the villages. They seek, as again they themselves say, *movimiento*, which might be translated as "progress." This pair of values and others which Dr. Lobo noted among the migrants explain a great deal concerning causes not only of the migration but also of the positive adaptation the barriada residents have made. This adaptation, too, is part of the picture which Dr. Lobo paints.

The value of this book lies in the fact that it is a full-length ethnography of the Peruvian barriada-dwellers, a balanced account of their social, economic, and religious life. Dr. Lobo brings us close to the people, presenting them as striving and sociable humans adapting to circumstances behind the facade of the squatter settlements in which they are forced to live. This study should be of great practical utility to social workers and city officials charged with improvement programs. It has grown out of the application of anthropology's simple, traditional method of participant observation. The high quality of the ethnography is a result not only of the sound method employed but also of the ethnographer's personal warmth and honest interest in the people of the barriadas.

EDWARD H. SPICER

ARRIVAL
IN
LIMA

On a clear summer day I could see from my plane window the vast Andes rising steeply above the coast of Peru, their immense presence overshadowing the narrow strip of coastal desert. Wind patterns in the sand were the desert's only visible features, except for the occasional rivers flowing from the mountains to the Pacific. Along these rivers were lush irrigated farmlands and the towns and cities where most of Peru's population is concentrated.

Migrations throughout the mountains and between the mountains and the coast have been an integral part of man's long history in the Andean region. The most recent migration began in the mid-1940s, as residents from the rural highlands moved to Lima and other industrializing cities to look for jobs. The first highlanders who came to the coast soon encouraged others to follow and the trickle of migration became a large stream. In the acute housing shortage which developed, thousands of migrants began to live in squatter settlements, or *barriadas:* by 1980 it was estimated that almost half the population of metropolitan Lima was living in squatter settlements.

The surge of migration to Lima has created numerous changes in the city itself. Often from the traditional Limeño's point of view, the large number of rural migrants threatens the cosmopolitan nature of the city. Many residents express not only a disdain for the *cholos* (highlanders of primarily Indian ancestry who have acquired some urban sophistication), but also a recurrent fear about the revolutionary potential of "the masses." The ambivalence felt by many urban Peruvians regarding the influx of migrants from rural regions is clearly expressed by the Peruvian writer Varallanos (1962:106):

> Today Lima is a city of *cholos,* that is, it has been cholified. . . .
> Thousands of indigenous peasants live in the so-called *"barriadas,"*
> or marginal neighborhoods. In effect, in these districts which,
> like mushrooms, have arisen in the outskirts of Lima as if to
> enclose it in a ring of misery and social promiscuity, live close
> to a half million *cholos* who each day give Lima a more Peruvian
> profile. It is this invasion of the capital by the highlanders from
> the forgotten provinces that is the revolution that humbly arrives
> at the gates of Lima without agitation or political demagogues
> . . . and continues to transform the republican and mestizo capital.*

Much has been written about squatter settlements. However, "a considerable amount of what has been written about such communities *(barriadas,* etc.) is based on little more than surface appearances, so there is a large corpus of myth which has only recently been challenged by those who have undertaken substantive research among the people in such communities" (Heath 1974:236). The description of life in the squatter settlements presented here is intended to document, ethnographically, the process of urbanization as it has occurred over a ten-year period in two residential areas of Lima and to correct the dearth of fundamental information regarding such vital areas as social structure, residence patterns, kinship, and values. In contrast to the negative picture so often found in the literature in which urbanization is viewed in terms of "breakdown," "disorganization," "marginality," or a "culture of poverty" model, the process of urbanization discussed here is an example of positive adaptation. That is, both from the migrants' point of view and from objective observation, certain criteria are met. These criteria can be described as the migrants' ability to build a community in both a material and a psychological sense,

---

*All translations from the original, except where otherwise noted, are by the author.

their achievement of goals such as education of children, access to urban amenities, and an increased income when compared to highland communities of origin and their positive view of themselves and of their future. Life in squatter settlements is by no means perfect or even easy, and it is evident that the migrants are existing in an extremely difficult and sometimes precarious situation in terms of obtaining the resources necessary for survival. Yet, from their viewpoint, they are succeeding.

The two communities where this study was carried out are Ciudadela Chalaca and Dulanto. They are located in the city of Callao, a part of the metropolitan Lima area. By government standards Dulanto is not considered a squatter settlement but rather an *urbanización popular* (housing development built by the people who live there), because the land is government-owned, the residents were settled by government initiative, and the possibility exists that title to individual lots may eventually go to the residents. On the other hand, prior to the government-sponsored "remodeling" in 1973, Ciudadela Chalaca was a squatter settlement that grew through the technically illegal initiative of the residents. After 1973 Ciudadela Chalaca became a squatter settlement in the process of remodeling, with some potential for resident ownership of individual lots.

I had originally intended to use pseudonyms for both Ciudadela Chalaca and Dulanto, in the anthropological tradition of protecting the anonymity of informants. However, because many informants requested that I include the names of their squatter settlements, I decided to refer here to both areas as they are known in Peru. I have, nevertheless, changed the names of all informants.

I first visited the squatter settlements of Lima in 1964 and lived in Ciudadela Chalaca for three months in 1965. I was able to establish some long-term friendships which were renewed four years later when I returned to Ciudadela Chalaca to live for four months in 1969. Returning in 1974 I lived with five different families, two in Dulanto and three in Ciudadela Chalaca, and began to understand what it is like to live every hour of the day in close quarters in an extremely dense population.

The actual choice of the individuals who compose the sample used in this study was the result of the interplay of a number of factors over the years in which contact has been maintained with the residents. Throughout the fieldwork I made an effort to maintain a sample which is representative of the families living in Ciudadela Chalaca and Dulanto in terms of site of origin in the highlands, age at migration, family composition, and economic and social involvement in urban life. The population in Ciudadela Chalaca and Dulanto is by no means homogeneous when observed in terms of such factors as these. Thus I made no attempt to fill this sample with "average" families; rather I tried to recognize and include in the sample the diverse types of families and individuals found in squatter settlements such as Ciudadela Chalaca and Dulanto.

ACKNOWLEDGMENTS

During the years of research and writing that produced this book, the encouragement and assistance of informants, colleagues, and friends has been extraordinary and genuinely appreciated. Throughout all stages of the study I have benefited enormously from the helpful critical advice of Edward Spicer, Constance Cronin, and Richard Henderson. Edward Spicer provided a constant source of inspiration, and his vision will, I am convinced, guide me throughout my life. I also wish to thank Keith Basso for his help during the early stages of this study. I am indebted to the numerous colleagues and fellow students with whom I discussed my ideas and enthusiasms. They gave me equal measures of critical advice and sympathy. They include Thomas Hinton, Patricia Lyon, John Rowe, Elizabeth Colsen, George Foster, Mac Chapin, David Cleveland, Alison MacEwan, and Billie Jean Isbell. I am particularly indebted to the Peruvian anthropologists Enrique Mayer and Luis Millones for the many stimulating conversations we shared. Some of the field expenses for this research were provided by grants from the Comins Fellowship Research Fund in 1969 and 1974. I wish to thank the University of Arizona Press for publishing this work.

I owe a particular debt of gratitude to my many friends and kinsmen who have provided me with their generous support, encouragement, and patience during the field research and the writing of this book. These kind folk include Randi Starmer, M. S. Remrats, John Kinevich, Camilla Kirkham, Patricia Whiteside, Judith Chafee, and Helen Jones. In addition, Rita Lobo and Ruth Lobo cared for my daughter while I was in the field in 1974, for which I shall be eternally grateful. I also wish to thank Frank Lobo for the years of kind understanding and encouragement that he provided during the preparation of this study and for his aid in the field in 1969 and during six weeks in 1974. I also want to express my appreciation for the patient understanding of my daughter, Kelina Lobo. I have been working on this book since the day she was born. To my mother, Mildred Bloom Parker, and my late father, Frank Bloom, I am forever indebted for their having instilled in me the independence, curiosity, and persistence that was necessary to complete this work.

Finally, I owe a very special and deep debt of gratitude to the many informants and friends living in the squatter settlements of Peru who generously contributed their time and energy to this research.

SUSAN LOBO

PART ONE

The Squatter Settlements

THE BARRIADA SETTING

CHAPTER 1

Approaching Lima from the air, one realizes with a start that what looks at first like a part of the surrounding desert is actually houses, thousands of them, arranged into a vast series of settlements. The visual impact is to many a visceral experience. Here are houses and neighborhoods with millions of people living in them, an immense population spreading over a vast expanse. In the center is downtown Lima with its tall buildings and paved streets, yet in area this traditional urban portion is engulfed and almost submerged in the mile after mile of less formal settlements. Some are irregularly and extremely densely settled; others are laid out in a grid pattern. Although these squatter settlements, or *barriadas*, take various forms, they share many characteristics. They are built by the people who live in them, and the vast majority of those residents are families which have migrated from the Andean highlands.

After landing at the airport, if one rides by car or bus on a major thoroughfare toward the central districts of Lima, there is a different perspective, but a continuation of the sensation that one is in the midst

[3]

A squatter settlement in Lima, Peru, in 1974, stretches as far as the eye can see.

of a heavily populated area. Stretching out from each side of the thoroughfare as far as the eye can see are houses and more houses, many of them contiguous, forming a solid wall along the road. Some of these houses are built with scrap lumber and woven mats, some with brick or other materials. There is almost no vegetation. Dirt roads and a few paved ones lead into the settlements. And there are people: thousands and thousands of people, on foot, in crowded buses, and in cars, creating a great deal of activity on the streets leading into downtown Lima.

Once inside a barriada one loses the awareness of the immensity of the settled area and becomes more aware of the particulars. The waves of sensations are powerful: the smell of the open sewers, the sounds of the pushcart vendors' calls and bells, the sight of houses crowded along narrow, winding alleys. But most memorable are the people: the woman who deftly prepares and sells food at the marketplace, the man who sharpens knives at a small portable stall, the group of children in school uniforms, the woman who laughs as she hoists her baby onto her back, the child running by on an errand, the young men on their way to soccer practice, the women at a water spigot washing clothes, and more, many more people.

Among middle-class and upper-class Limeños, squatter settlements are often stereotyped as harboring criminals and social degenerates. It is believed that anyone from the outside who dares to walk through a squatter settlement would be lucky to escape with his life. Certain squatter settlements, among them Ciudadela Chalaca, are particularly renowned by outsiders for extreme depravity. The one social worker, whose territory included Ciudadela Chalaca, confided that she had only entered the squatter settlement a few times and then,

through fear of being accosted, was accompanied by a male colleague. She added, "The people there are too lazy and degenerate to warrant or appreciate help anyway." A Peruvian woman anthropologist, who was knowledgeable and sympathetic to the plight of those living in the squatter settlements, nevertheless expressed surprise that I was living in one and asked, "Isn't it too dangerous?" The regional school director, who chided parents from Ciudadela Chalaca for sending their children to school poorly dressed and ill-fed, said, "They will remain ignorant all of their lives." A nun expressed her belief that the prime interest of these people was sex and that she had heard that every man had a number of wives.

Stereotyping of squatter settlements has not been avoided by the residents themselves. In Ciudadela Chalaca young children and teenagers are warned to stay away from another squatter settlement two blocks distant because "cut-throats" live there. When a sociological article which mentions another well-known squatter settlement was brought to the attention of a number of Ciudadela Chalaca residents, the general response was that the author was insane to have dealt with those people, who are all "untrustworthy." Distance-maintaining mechanisms are prevalent even between different squatter settlements.

Influenced by these stereotypes, a visitor's first impression of squatter settlements, as has been expressed vividly by various popular and academic writers, is one of chaos, foul odors, and squalor. It is not until one begins to discern the rich complexity of interpersonal relationships; to see the multitude of patterns emerging from such aspects as marriage rules, residence patterns, and kin obligations; to understand the meaning of calling a squatter settlement home; and to make friends oneself that there is an incipient appreciation of the significance

[5]

of the nature of a squatter settlement, both for those who live there and for purposes of analysis. Although the surroundings may seem bleak, the people who live in the squatter settlements are not.

CIUDADELA CHALACA

Until the 1930s the site of Ciudadela Chalaca was an area of scattered small farms. A few farmers raised goats, milk cows, or pigs in addition to cultivating small plots of land. The area was on the outskirts of the port of Callao, and the street that becomes San Agustín was one of the thoroughfares for foot and burro travelers who brought their agricultural products to the Callao market. The open sewers that until 1973 ran through Ciudadela Chalaca were once irrigation ditches.

In 1938 five nuclear families migrated from the highland town of Corongo in Ancash and rented lots in the area which later became Ciudadela Chalaca. This group of first families built their homes with the traditional coastal cane and adobe. They dug shallow wells and had space for vegetable gardens and some stock. They called their small settlement Corongo Chico, a name which in 1974 was occasionally still used to refer to Ciudadela Chalaca. More families from Corongo came to the area and either rented other lots or built their houses on the lots of kin who were already established.

Ciudadela Chalaca grew by increments, unlike the many barriadas which were populated overnight through organized "invasions." In the early 1940s, however, two factors created an increase in the speed of settlement. In 1940 a large earthquake left many persons living in Callao homeless and also provided these same persons with access to building materials found in the rubble of destroyed buildings. Numerous families who had lost their houses in the earthquake moved to Corongo Chico and rented space from the original families and built their own houses. Many of those who moved to the area after the earthquake were *zambos* (people of black and Indian ancestry) or other *criollos* (long-time urban residents) who established the core of the nonmigrant population of Ciudadela Chalaca. During the Second World War increased industrialization stimulated a surge of migration from the rural highlands. As the population in Ciudadela Chalaca of both migrants from the highlands and criollos from central Callao increased, the density likewise increased, leaving little room for the vegetable gardens and stock-raising of a few years before.

In 1953 the Ciudadela Chalaca was granted limited recognition by the government, and a community council was appointed by the residents. This body was given the title *"Asociación Urbanizadora de los Poseedores de Ciudadela Chalaca"* ("Urbanizing Association of Possessors of Ciudadela Chalaca"). As this title suggests, the community council represents individuals who are in possession of Ciudadela Chalaca but who do not officially own it. The title to the property was officially in litigation.

In 1961 the recognition of Ciudadela Chalaca as an official *barrio marginal* (marginal district) by the government allowed the "possessors" to receive the benefits of public law #13517. This law, at least in theory, specified that Ciudadela Chalaca was to receive the municipal benefits of police protection and garbage collection. Both the 1953 formation of the community council and the 1961 recognition of Ciudadela Chalaca increased the strength of the residents' claim to the land.

In 1973 a government-initiated "remodeling" process was begun. The project was implemented through SINAMOS (Sistema Nacional de Apoyo a la Movilización Social) with the explicit goal of decreasing density, regularizing lot size, and making water, sewer, and electricity available to each lot. Also, arrangements were to be made for each household eventually to gain legal title to its lot. The remodeling of Ciudadela Chalaca during this period was part of a city-wide policy to encourage self-help house construction within the squatter settlements. By 1974 a portion of Ciudadela Chalaca had been demolished, and some of the residents of this razed area were assigned lots that had been laid out to form the future city blocks. These lots did not yet have electricity, water or utilities, and the families who settled here rebuilt houses of scrap lumber and matting that were similar to those found in Ciudadela Chalaca prior to the remodeling. Some households, designated *excedentes*, were settled in the still-standing older sections of Ciudadela Chalaca. Other households were given the option of obtaining a lot in the nearby relocation site that was to become the community of Dulanto.

By 1980 the remodeling had only partially met the original goals. Utilities were available to some of the lots that had been established at the time of the first stages of the remodeling. A number of households were still in the process of obtaining legal title to their lots, while others had been unsuccessful in obtaining title. Many households, particularly those in which land title was secured, had proceeded to construct houses of brick and cement. Other houses remained as before the remodeling. Also a substantial number of excedentes continued to live in irregular-sized lots without utilities or title to their lots. One resident remarked, "What was to have been temporary, has

A comparatively wide walkway in Ciudadela Chalaca
in 1965 is lined with houses constructed primarily of
woven reed matting and irregular wood boards.

become perpetual." In 1980 Ciudadela Chalaca presented the face of a
community in the process of slow change, with portions and segments
reflecting distinct points along a continuum of the history of the
community.

Ciudadela Chalaca is located in Lima's port, Callao, in a mixed
industrial and lower-middle-class district. It is bounded on the south
by the main thoroughfare, Avenida Argentina, and on the west by the
street Contralmirante Mora. To the north are the squatter settlement
San Juan Bosco and a series of railroad tracks and loading areas. To
the east are high cement walls surrounding a number of factories.
Ciudadela Chalaca is within walking distance of the seaside docks.
Until the remodeling in 1973 one entered the settlement from Avenida

It is common for families to have pets as a part of the
household. Pigs, as well as dogs, may be named and
raised with kindness; however, the pig will eventually
be slaughtered for a fiesta meal.

Argentina, crossing one of a series of small wood or cement bridges
under which flowed what appeared to be a slowly moving stream.
The running water added a quaint, pastoral aspect to the urban setting. On closer inspection, however, one quickly realized that the
stream was actually an open sewer. The street of San Agustín, which
was about sixty feet wide, ran down the middle of the settlement. The
other sectors were connected by a labyrinth of narrow and twisted
pathways which led past contiguous housefronts. Millones (1975:59)
aptly describes the external appearance of a similar squatter settlement as filled with "twisting alleyways similar to those found in a
medieval city."

Before the remodeling in 1973 some areas in Ciudadela Chalaca were open to the public as thoroughfares, and public buildings and facilities were located there. Other areas were more private in nature with foot traffic limited to those living in the immediate area or to those with business in the area. Certain areas were filled with clusters of *paisanos* (migrants from the same highland district) or smaller kin and sibling groups. San Agustín was the main street in Ciudadela Chalaca and many commercial businesses as well as the school and medical post were located along it; a number of mobile vendors also plied their trades there. San Agustín was also crossed by a number of narrower but also frequently traveled passageways. The community council officially divided Ciudadela Chalaca into sectors which often corresponded to the divisions which resulted from the crosscutting of larger passageways. The small passageways generally have no official names but may be locally known as, for example, *"Callejón del Diablo"* ("Devil's Passageway") or *"Callejón del Cariño"* ("Lover's Lane").

Prior to the remodeling I had estimated that there were at least 12,000 people living in the approximately nine hectares that comprise Ciudadela Chalaca, with a density of about 553 persons per acre. The Oficina Nacional de Estadística y Censos (1974c:173) estimated a population of 9,188 for Ciudadela Chalaca. Aside from the human population, almost every household includes a dog that serves as both a pet and a watchdog. Many households also raise guinea pigs, ducks, rabbits, and even goats, sheep, and pigs.

HOUSING

In 1964 the majority of the houses had one story and were constructed of *esteras* (woven reed matting). Some were constructed of irregular wood boards, and a very few were of brick or cement. In 1955 Matos found that in Ciudadela Chalaca "99 percent of the houses are constructed of wood, esteras or other flammable materials, while 1 percent are constructed of adobe" (1966b:41). By 1969 there was a more substantial type of construction. The majority of the houses previously constructed of esteras had been rebuilt of wood, and many others were constructed of brick and cement. Wood and bricks had been gathered from the rubble of buildings in Callao which were destroyed in the 1967 earthquake. Most residents of Ciudadela Chalaca think of an earthquake not as a disaster personally but as an opportunity to take advantage of free building materials. Quite a few residents had built second stories of esteras onto their homes for sleeping rooms. Most houses grew by increments as families were able to acquire funds for building materials or were able to salvage material.

By 1974, after the remodeling, those families that had been placed on lots within the area of Ciudadela Chalaca had reconstructed temporary homes similar to those I had first observed in 1964. Residents were reluctant to construct sturdier and more expensive houses until official governmental permission to build was given. The families that had remained in the areas of Ciudadela Chalaca that were not yet divided into uniform lots again built temporary homes of wood and esteras as they waited to hear where the government would eventually place them. Almost without exception, the houses built of adobe, brick, or cement before the remodeling were razed when the remodeling began.

The homes in Ciudadela Chalaca both prior to and after the remodeling range from those of one dimly lit room to those that consist of a number of comfortably furnished rooms. Whenever possible the downstairs area is divided into at least two rooms, the living room and the kitchen-dining area, both of which may also contain beds. If a family decides to lay a wood or cement floor, the kitchen area is generally the last room to be thus floored. Interior lighting is provided either from small glassless windows with interior shutters which are closed at night or from overhead skylights, which also may be closed at night.

Furniture is generally simple and utilitarian, the basic items being a wooden table, chairs, and a bed. However, as soon as a family has sufficient resources, one of its necessary purchases is a "parlor set," which consists of a wood-frame overstuffed sofa and matching straight-backed wooden chairs. The sofa and chairs are generally covered with clear plastic. Occasionally an end table and lamp or a wooden cupboard is included. (A similar desire for a parlor set in the slums of Venezuela is described by Peattie 1970:17.) The parlor set is placed to one side of the living room or in a partitioned area. It is used primarily when the family receives guests and is felt to be necessary by those families which aspire to middle-class status.

Pictures cut out of magazines and family photographs — of babies, of children in their class pictures, of a young girl at her first communion, or of the wedding of the parents of the household — are hung on the wall. Occasionally the elementary school diploma of one or more of the children or of the parents will be displayed. The rare saint's picture is of San Martín de Porres or San Pedro, the two most popular saints. A number of homes have electric lighting. Many families have radios and an increasing number have televisions.

A typically well-organized kitchen will most likely
have a kerosene stove for cooking like the one shown
here on the left. The basket used for shopping hangs
from the rafter. The stone on the table near the
cooking pots is a "pestle" used for grinding.

The kitchen is usually the area where there is the least evidence
of modernization. A few women cook over small fires, though the
majority have primus or kerosene stoves with one or two burners.
The kitchen usually has a table used as a cutting surface and a place
for storage. Utensils are hung on walls or on cords strung overhead.
As food is purchased daily, there is no need for a refrigerator, although
some families buy one as a prestige item. Water is brought from the
nearest outdoor spigot and stored in a bucket or cistern. The cooking
is such that there are few food scraps. However, greens that are

trimmed are usually dropped on the floor for the rabbits or guinea pigs which are often raised in the kitchen. Goats, sheep, or a pig may be in a small open courtyard and fed scraps. The kitchen is a model of maximum utilization of resources: there is very little that is wasted or thrown away. Tin cans are used for storage or in patching the house; boxes, paper, and bottles are saved and reused or sold.

The sleeping rooms contain a number of cots or beds, usually with straw mattresses. Clothing is hung across overhead lines or poles or is placed in cardboard boxes or wooden trunks. Occasionally a family has an upright wooden wardrobe.

The houses in Ciudadela Chalaca bespeak of utilitarian simplicity. Except for the parlor area, the homes are arranged for convenience and economy. The average household in my sample consisted of slightly more than six permanent members who were often joined by short- or long-term visitors. The primary function of each house is to provide an eating and sleeping area for this number of individuals. The houses are arranged with an eye toward what is absolutely necessary to provide these services; further embellishments are added only as each household finds them economically efficient.

PUBLIC AND COMMERCIAL FACILITIES

Prior to remodeling in 1973 there existed in Ciudadela Chalaca a number of community-wide facilities. There were five *caños*, or watering areas, located in Ciudadela Chalaca in 1964. In 1969 there were fourteen; after the remodeling there were nine. Caños are cement basins with two to four water spigots and a drain area; all of the water used in the homes of Ciudadelo Chalaca is obtained from them. In the mornings and early evenings there are lines of people waiting to obtain water. During the slack periods of the day, late morning and early afternoon, women use these caño areas to wash their hair, launder the family's clothing, and bathe their children. Adults give themselves sponge baths in the privacy of their homes. The caño water is not potable and is boiled before being consumed. Each caño has a different history; however, most were built through the cooperative effort of the residents of a particular sector of Ciudadela Chalaca. In a few instances, some materials or funds were supplied by the state welfare agency or the Catholic church. All labor and most materials were supplied by the residents. The caños drain into the open sewers which run throughout the barriada, the same sewers into which the contents of the night pots are dumped.

Electricity was obtained by about half of the households between 1967 and 1977. Most other households use kerosene or candles for lighting. Residents who live near the main public thoroughfares have little problem in obtaining electric service from the electric companies. They often rent electricity to their neighbors who live farther from the main streets. Others pirate electricity from power poles running along the main thoroughfares or from nearby municipal buildings. Often groups of neighbors or extended families form cooperatives for obtaining and distributing electric power. The details of the formation of this type of cooperative have been well described by Frank Lobo (1970).

Since 1963 garbage has been collected in Ciudadela Chalaca once a week. A large municipal truck enters at one end and drives along the one passable street, collecting garbage left in containers by the residents. This procedure seems to be reasonably effective, for one rarely sees organic material or trash of any kind anywhere in Ciudadela Chalaca. However, this fact seems to be due as much to the dogs and the residents' ability to use everything until it has absolutely disintegrated as it is to the garbage collectors.

Until the remodeling in 1973 one soccer field existed in Ciudadela Chalaca and a number of others were located on the periphery. These fields were used by the local soccer teams for their weekly Sunday matches. The fields themselves were guarded zealously from new squatters by the households living adjacent to them. With the remodeling all but one of the soccer fields were subdivided into lots.

According to the Peruvian Constitution (Articles 72 and 73), a school must be provided for an area in which there are at least thirty school-age children. Therefore Ciudadela Chalaca has one public elementary school. It consists of eight rooms and employs six teachers. The boys attend in the morning, girls in the afternoon, and adult education is conducted in the evenings. Most parents show an interest in their children's education. All youths living in the barriada who attend high schools must attend those in downtown Callao. Five small schools, the equivalent of preschools or nursery schools, are run by women in their homes in Ciudadela Chalaca.

Prior to the remodeling Ciudadela Chalaca had a small two-room medical post run by the Callao Public Health Department. Since attending doctors donated their time, their schedules were often erratic and on many days the post was not open. However, a small pharmacy run by a family living in the barriada has a fairly steady stream of customers. The owner is certified to make injections and in many ways acts in a paramedical fashion. At the time of remodeling the medical post was removed, but in 1974 the pharmacy continued to function and three women living nearby had learned how to make injections.

Before 1967 there was no police station in Ciudadela Chalaca, and residents were left to their own devices as far as crime control was concerned. Because of the residence pattern of relatives living near one another, the fact that all residents are known to one another, and the strong effectiveness of gossip and social pressure, there is a low crime rate in Ciudadela Chalaca. Crimes of violence are very rare; only one murder was remembered by informants. Mothers show no reluctance to send their young children and teenage daughters on errands after dark. The professional thieves who live in Ciudadela Chalaca carry out their business activities elsewhere, particularly in the affluent areas of the city. While they are in the settlement, their behavior conforms to the expectations of the other residents. The most recurrent crimes are wife-beatings and sneak thievery. Teenage boys who live in Ciudadela Chalaca occasionally break into unlocked houses and steal items.

In 1967 a group of residents petitioned the mayor of Callao to establish a police post. The city donated the materials, and the labor for the construction was supplied by a group of residents. The police post is located at the extreme edge of Ciudadela Chalaca and was untouched by the remodeling. One policeman is usually stationed in the post. Many informants complain that the police still do not patrol and "are very lazy."

A large cement dining hall was constructed in Ciudadela Chalaca in 1963 with United States Alliance for Progress funds. Until the building was torn down at the time of the remodeling, a free breakfast was served by Callao public health workers to all the children attending the local school. As the school became crowded, the dining hall was divided into four rooms in which classes were held. At the end of one room was a small altar. On Sundays a Catholic priest occasionally gave a mass in this room, though it was never attended by more than forty people. Generally, the residents of Ciudadela Chalaca demonstrate little concern for church attendance. The two outer walls of a half-finished church stood in Ciudadela Chalaca for years until they were demolished at the time of the remodeling.

Ciudadela Chalaca also had a meeting hall, the *local*, which was constructed through communal effort in 1953. Besides being the site for weekly community council meetings, the building was used for adult education classes in electricity, literacy, and sewing, and for occasional dances which the community council sponsored. The meeting hall was also removed at the time of the remodeling, but a temporary structure was constructed nearby to replace it.

Commercial facilities in Ciudadela Chalaca are notable for their small scale and their sheer numbers. Almost every family is involved in at least one commercial venture, a situation similar to the "urban penny capitalism," observed by Anthony Leeds in the squatter settlements of Brazil (personal communication, 1971). A daily market unaffected by the remodeling is held in the open air at the southwest corner of Ciudadela Chalaca. The sales areas range from small permanent wooden stalls, to pushcarts or flat trays on sawhorses, to goods laid on a piece of cloth spread on the ground. In 1964 there was an average of 134 vendors. By 1969 there averaged 310 and this number remained the same in 1974. Among those items for sale are fresh produce, meat, and fish, as well as dry goods, fruit, clothing, toys, cooking utensils, and curing herbs.

Within Ciudadela Chalaca itself there are a number of small housefront stores and enterprises. In a typical two-block stretch are seven dry-goods stores, two shoe-repair shops, two bars, four prepared-food stands, one soccer clubhouse, one political club, and one pharmacy. The prices at these small stores are slightly higher than at the local markets, but their more convenient location makes up for the difference.

A number of temporary stalls often appear on the streets for a few weeks and then vanish as the owners become involved in other enterprises. Vendors may repair shoes or sell fruit or hot teas prepared at night. Working with one such vendor of fried sweetbread for three days, I observed that her monetary intake was only slightly higher than her economic investment. However, she gave many breads to her neighbors, relatives, and fictive kin, thereby activating in her favor the scale of social reciprocity. She also enhanced her reputation as a hard-working woman.

Additionally, a number of ambulatory vendors pass through Ciudadela Chalaca, each with a characteristic whistle, bell, or call to identify his or her approach. The most conspicuous are the bread vendors, who come in the morning shortly before seven and in the evening at dusk. Many bread vendors who live in the squatter settlements ply their trade outside of it, selling the remaining bread on their way home after work. A number of candy and cookie vendors pass along the walkways of Ciudadela Chalaca and often station themselves outside the local elementary school. Knife sharpeners are often seen. On Sundays barbers who live in Ciudadela Chalaca, but who ply their trade elsewhere during the week, walk through the area carrying their chairs and some comic books. At times a professional photographer passes through the settlement carrying his large black camera and a wooden horse used as a prop in taking children's photographs. Occasionally "Turks," or Gypsies, sell their assorted goods.

A credit cooperative and two housing cooperatives were formed in the mid-1960s and operated until the early 1970s. The credit cooperative was controlled by the community council. Monthly dues were collected from the members and deposited in a city bank. Ideally, loans are extended to members from this capital. By 1969, according to members, this cooperative was functioning satisfactorily. Two housing cooperatives existed in Ciudadela Chalaca prior to the remodeling. The members pooled their money with the eventual aim of buying a tract of land on the outskirts of Lima. When the remodeling occurred, however, most members withdrew their funds to use for individual house construction.

POSSESSION OF HOMES AND LAND

Many squatter settlements in Lima were established clandestinely and grew literally overnight (Mangin 1967a; Reategui 1971). In contrast, Ciudadela Chalaca grew through a slow process of accretion lasting more than thirty years. Most squatter settlements that were established through invasion have lots of uniform size while those that grew through accretion often do not. The lots of Ciudadela Chalaca until the 1973 remodeling were quite irregular in shape and size.

In Ciudadela Chalaca most houses grow by increments as the family members acquire funds to buy building materials or are able to salvage them, and as space for construction becomes available. In most phases of house construction both men and women may be active, although the labor of men predominates. For example, Celsa and Jorge and their three-year-old son had lived in Ciudadela Chalaca in the home of Jorge's sister since migrating to Lima two years previously. Although they had saved only a small amount of cash since their arrival, Celsa and Jorge nevertheless could expect help from a large network of kin and paisanos who lived in their residential cluster. Jorge's sister was particularly eager to help her brother construct his own house. One night, with the help of the sister, the sister's husband, and Jorge's brother, the couple placed esteras at both ends of a twelve-foot-wide passageway between two houses, thus creating the end walls of a twelve-by-fifteen-foot house. Although by this date (1969) it was against the general policy established by the elected community council for new houses to be constructed in the already reduced open areas of Ciudadela Chalaca, most of their kin and paisanos were well aware of what had occurred, were sympathetic to Celsa and Jorge's plan, and were prepared to support their action. As one paisano, Domatilda, said, "We don't really need that little passageway. And besides, they should at least have a house of their own."

The day after the construction of the end walls, an official from the community council visited Celsa and Jorge in their new house. The kin who had helped them the night before were present, as was Celsa's aunt, who also had a house nearby. Before the community official entered their house, the aunt tried to dissuade him, saying that it was not a house at all, but a chicken coop that she and her husband were building. Although both the aunt and the official were well aware of the true nature of the construction, the aunt's argument was a symbolic gesture of kin support and solidarity for Celsa and Jorge. The problem was resolved when the young couple paid the official for a permit to build. Following the official's visit, Celsa and Jorge moved their bed, a bench, a table, her cooking equipment, and their clothing into their house. His siblings and her aunt then gave them some scrap lumber and bricks to replace the esteras.

By evening their house presented a facade not unlike those of their immediate neighbors. The esteras were placed on the roof until the following weekend, when Jorge purchased enough lumber to finish half of the roof. The floor was left sod, as is done in many houses. Their house, while modest by squatter-settlement standards, provided adequate space for the family to sleep and to prepare and eat their food. Two months after the house was constructed, Celsa's younger sister, the sister's husband, and their four small children moved to Lima from their home community in the highlands and joined Celsa and Jorge in their house for eight months. The sister bought five esteras, and her husband constructed a sleeping room for his family on the roof, which they reached by a wooden ladder through an open hatch. All nine members of the newly formed household shared cooking and eating facilities. Cages for chickens were then built on the portion of the roof not covered by the sleeping room. Small shelters for guinea pigs were also placed around the walls of the kitchen area. This process of expansion is typical of many of the houses in Ciudadela Chalaca.

That Celsa and Jorge made the first step of their house construction and laid claim to the property at night is significant. If an individual is able to construct a house at night without detection, by the following morning when the construction is discovered his squatter's rights are almost equal to those of the other "possessors" of lots in Ciudadela Chalaca. A united group of paisanos and kin is also helpful in forestalling immediate detection of new construction by the community officials. In Ciudadela Chalaca the community council has no clear and consistent sanctioning power, but only the power given to it through the consent of the residents. An individual undertaking new construction will usually manage to build the new house if he or she has numerous kin residing in the same sector of the squatter settlement who will exert enough influence to prevent any neighbor's complaint to the community council. By 1969, however, the virtual absence of unused ground space dictated that any further expansion would be upward to second stories.

A group of five well-organized siblings and their spouses constructed a house in another manner common in Ciudadela Chalaca (two of the siblings' spouses were first cousins of the houseowner's wife, Fernandina). José and Fernandina decided to remodel their poorly constructed, one-story house built of scrap lumber and esteras. Additional lumber was obtained through the kin network. All five of the siblings and their spouses and some of the children of these couples began to work early Sunday morning, tearing the old structure to the ground, removing the nails from the old boards, and then reconstructing a sturdy, two-room wooden house by late afternoon. By evening, the major portion of the interior was completed, as was a second-story sleeping room. The furniture was returned to the newly built house that same night.

During the day the householders provided beer for those who helped in the construction. Fernandina also prepared an elaborate midday meal for them with the help of her sister. In the evening the house was baptized with the breaking of a bottle of champagne by the *madrina* (godmother) of the new house, who was Fernandina's sister. A relatively modest party followed, in which another meal and beer were served to those who had participated in the construction, followed by dancing to recorded music. The following weekend, José and Fernandina painted the interior. As is traditional, the mental tally of give and take was carefully maintained by each individual who participated in this particular construction effort. Reciprocity of materials and labor was expected when the necessity arose. This example of house remodeling is somewhat similar to the descriptions (such as in Mayer 1977) of mutual aid in house construction as found in the Andean highlands. In this case, however, as the house was easily disassembled and rebuilt, the actual construction time was reduced and the project was completed in one day of concentrated effort.

Within squatter settlements a vast range of possibilities exists regarding ownership of land; from outright legal renting, to renting with various arrangements of tenuous ownership or future potential ownership, to installment-buying of land, to outright and effective ownership of land by the residents. Since 1961 the families living in Ciudadela Chalaca have been referred to, and refer to themselves, as "possessors" of Ciudadela Chalaca (see Ley de las Barriadas [1961], and Smith [1964] for clarification of this law). By 1974 lot payment had not begun and the residents remained possessors. House construction in Ciudadela Chalaca in 1974 was temporary, as residents awaited some security of land title before investing in permanent construction.

ETHNIC DIVERSITY

Two common refrains heard in Ciudadela Chalaca and Dulanto indicate something of ethnic variation and stereotypes.

*La peor cosa que le puede ocurrir es que un cholo tenga mando,
un negro tenga plata, y un blanco sea pobre.*

The worst thing that can happen is that a *cholo* takes command, a black has money, and a white is poor.

*Tus ojos son luceros,
Tu boca es un corral,
Por eso, bajaste del cielo,
Cholo, bruto y animal.*

Your eyes are lamps,
Your mouth is a corral,
Because of this you came down from heaven,
cholo, brute and animal.

[children's refrain said by criollos to cholos]

In Ciudadela Chalaca there are two sharply defined populations: the migrants from the highlands and the *criollos*. This squatter settlement is ethnically less homogeneous than many others. Traditionally Callao, as a coastal city and a port, has had a predominantly coastal and urban population.

The term *criollo* has many different definitions, depending on situation and social class. In the squatter settlements it is most generally used to designate people who were born on the coast and are adept with urban coastal forms of behavior. Most of the criollos living in Ciudadela Chalaca and Dulanto are also *zambos,* that is, of mixed black, white, and Indian ancestry. Zambos are typically coastal people culturally and are characterized by a sharp wit and smooth talk. From the point of view of the highland migrants, they are the epitome of the city slicker: the most criollo of the criollo. They are generally of low income and tend to live in the old districts of metropolitan Lima. However, some live in squatter settlements as well. In many respects the zambos are in direct competition with the migrants from the highlands for employment, housing, and facilities such as hospitals and schools which are intended for low-income groups.

In Ciudadela Chalaca those who would classify themselves as criollos or zambos represent approximately one third of the population. In Dulanto zambos are less numerous, representing no more than one tenth of the population. Because of Ciudadela Chalaca's location in Callao in an area of traditionally heavy zambo population, this squatter settlement has a characteristically higher proportion of zambos than many of the other squatter settlements located in the foothills to the north and south of Lima. Within Ciudadela Chalaca ethnic residential clustering was evident until the remodeling in 1973. As the squatter settlement grew, highlanders consistently moved in with highlanders, and zambos moved in with zambos. The interaction between the highlanders and the zambos is expressed by an entire gamut of responses, from close friendships and *compadre* relationships to smouldering hostility, but generally is characterized by cautious distance.

POLITICAL ORGANIZATION

In reference to the remodeling of Ciudadela Chalaca in 1973, one young man remarked, "This place was so well-organized before. All the government did was to succeed in disorganizing it." He was referring to the community council that had governed Ciudadela Chalaca from 1953. The following officers were elected annually.

Secretaría general	Chairman
Secretaría de economía	Treasurer
Secretaría de actas	Secretary/recorder
Secretaría de deporte	Secretary of Sports
Secretaría de cultura	Secretary of Cultural Events

Secretaría de cooperativos	Secretary of Cooperatives
Secretaría de defensa	Secretary of Defense
Secretaría de disciplina	Secretary of Discipline
Fiscal	Secretary to keep order during meetings
Asistenta Social	Secretary of Social welfare

Votes were cast by heads of households who were "official" possessors of lots in Ciudadela Chalaca. Length of residence usually was the factor that changed one from "unofficial" to "official." Except for the asistenta social and the secretaría de cultura, who most often were women, the elected officials were usually chosen from among a group of men in their late forties and fifties. A ruling clique was created since offices tended to rotate from one man to another.

The community council serves functions both internal and external to the squatter settlement. Within the squatter settlement it organizes community-wide events such as dances. It also has limited power to stop construction of new houses in sectors that are judged overcrowded. However, this power was often informally overruled by the members of a residential paisano and kin cluster. The community council also acts as a liaison and buffer between the squatter settlement and the outside world. Community council members successfully solicited from government agencies sufficient materials to complete construction of three new water spigots in 1969. For many years they petitioned a variety of government agencies in an attempt to clear titles to the land for the residents who lived there. It is the community council which approves events such as a political speech or a street performance by a university acting troupe, or that allows an outsider such as an anthropologist to take up residence in the squatter settlement. Funds for community projects are often obtained by council members through persistent petitioning of ministries, welfare agencies, and ultimately the establishment of personal contacts with individuals with influence in government agencies. Often national political figures find it advantageous to extend their support to a populous squatter settlement.

After 1973 SINAMOS, the government agency in charge of the remodeling, determined that three delegates (Coordinador, Secretaría de Economía, and the Fiscal) would be elected from each block, and these delegates would then choose the community-wide Secretaría General, Secretaría de Organización, Secretaría de Cultura, and Secretaría de Economía. However, by 1974, because of the large number of excedentes (residents who did not qualify for permanent lots) who were not living in blocks, organizational structure was viewed by the residents as transitional, and community-wide election of the four officers named above still took place. In addition, the excedentes had formed a nonsanctional governing body that functioned primarily to express to government agencies and the official community council their dissatisfaction with their having excedente classification.

At the same time as the remodeling a formal, community-wide youth group, *el Club Juvenil,* was formed that fulfilled both a social and a parapolitical function. It had 150 members, about 70 of whom were active. Many of the leaders of this club had, as young teenagers in 1964, been members of a Red Cross club introduced by a Peace Corps volunteer. By 1974 many of the leaders of the youth club were attending college and were more aware of national political issues than most adults living in Ciudadela Chalaca. They also took an interest in community issues, and the community council allowed one of their members to sit as a nonvoting member at council meetings. In 1974 el Club Juvenil organized and carried out two community-wide events: a volleyball tournament and a variety show for Mother's Day.

In Dulanto, the relocation settlement sponsored by the government, the manner of organization was the same one designated by SINAMOS for Ciudadela Chalaca. Four delegates from each block were elected to attend the council meetings, and at these meetings the council officials were elected. The council was to meet twice a week, but because this arrangement proved difficult for the members, the meetings were reduced to once a week in 1974. In Dulanto the community council functions primarily to relay the needs of the community to SINAMOS. However, internal complaints of a community nature are often given to the council for arbitration. Because of the strong role taken by SINAMOS in the affairs of Dulanto, the community council plays a less autonomous role than in Ciudadela Chalaca. It is interesting to note that Dulanto, a community with a great deal of dynamic construction and idealistic orientation toward future goals, first elected a comparatively young community council, the president of which was only thirty-two. By the winter of 1974 a number of older men had been elected to the council, although the president was a man in his thirties.

EDUCATION

One of the reasons highlanders move to the city is to obtain educations for their children. Adults who have migrated from the highlands, who have had a minimum of formal education themselves, view education as one of the most feasible routes of upward mobility for their children. The Oficina Nacional de Estadística y Censos (1972: 23b) found in a survey of squatter settlements of Callao made in 1970 that the educational levels were:

	Men	Women
Primary or less	62%	61%
Secondary	31%	20%
Post-secondary	2%	1%
No answer	5%	18%

A small survey carried out by the Area de Salud de Callao (1964) among residents of all ages in Ciudadela Chalaca reveals similar figures:

Primary	56%
Secondary	10%
University	0%
Technical	5%
No formal education	6%
No response	4%
Less than eight years of age	23%

The most notable change in the next ten years was that many young people began studies in technical schools and universities. Among the adults living in Ciudadela Chalaca and Dulanto who have migrated from the highlands, there is a tendency for the men to have had somewhat more formal education than the women. Many adult women living in Ciudadela Chalaca and Dulanto spoke bitterly of their own childhoods and their parents' lack of foresight or inability to send them to school when they were children. Domatilda said, ". . . but I am going to see that all of my girls go to school." Her two oldest children are attending the public secondary school and are learning technical trades, and the four younger ones attend primary school. Although not all families living in Ciudadela Chalaca and Dulanto are able to afford the luxury of keeping their high-school-aged children out of the labor force and in school, many do manage to send their children to secondary school, and many more with small children express a desire to do so. In the squatter settlements, where there is a high value placed on hard work for practical ends, the residents see quite clearly that those who are trained in technical skills in an industrial nation receive higher pay than the unskilled. Thus, the parents' educational goals for their children are not the upper-middle-class professions but the skilled jobs in the industrial or commercial sectors.

Parents instill in their children a strong drive to acquire an education. The young woman pictured wanted to be a school teacher from the time she was fourteen. By 1974, she had been teaching for three years.

In 1964 Ciudadela Chalaca had one elementary school located on the main street of San Agustín. Another school located adjacent to Ciudadela Chalaca in the small squatter settlement of San Juan Bosque was also attended by many children living in Ciudadela Chalaca. The schools remained intact during the remodeling of 1973 and continued to function as before.

The school in Ciudadela Chalaca includes eight classrooms plus a small library, office, and central courtyard. Prior to 1969 the girls attended in the afternoons and the boys attended in the mornings. In 1969 the use of the school was shifted so that girls attended in the mornings and boys in the afternoons. According to the teaching personnel this shift was brought about so that the children would spend more time doing their homework. Prior to this shift most girls shopped for food and helped prepare the midday meal before going to school, while the boys often had afternoon jobs. In Dulanto there is one primary school of six classrooms. In keeping with the educational reform policy initiated in the early 1970s, boys and girls attend school together. However, the school day is still split with some of the children attending in the morning and the others in the afternoon.

All of the teachers in the elementary school of Ciudadela Chalaca and Dulanto are urban and middle class in orientation and live outside the squatter settlements. Only on exceptional occasions do they have contact with the families of the children whom they teach — it is the rare teacher who has visited his or her students' homes. There are two exceptions, however. One of the first-grade teacher's aides was a resident of Ciudadela Chalaca who had previously taught preschool in her home, and a fourth-grade teacher was born and spent much of his youth in Ciudadela Chalaca, returning to teach there once he had obtained his degree.

Most parent participation in the school is through a formal *Padres de Familia* (parents' organization) that meets two or three times per semester. The Padres de Familia in Ciudadela Chalaca paid for and installed exterior lighting around the school, raised money for the school band instruments, and purchased and set up the school library. It is the responsibility of the government to provide the instructors, but each district or squatter settlement must provide the school building, the desks, and the supplies. It is through the Padres de Familia that the physical plant was constructed and maintained. Funds raised through raffles and street parties pay for additional school equipment. In Ciudadela Chalaca and Dulanto a custodian is paid by the families of children in attendance to clean and handle minor repairs in the school building. Major repairs and repainting are taken care of by the fathers of the children on the weekends when they are freed from their regular employment.

Sending a child to public elementary school represents a relatively expensive undertaking for a family living in Ciudadela Chalaca or Dulanto. Each child must wear the official school uniform. Children must also supply their own textbooks and school equipment. Additional expenses accrue if the child has a special project or keeps a project notebook, if the class takes a field trip, or if the child has to participate in a school pageant that requires a special outfit. Most families living in the squatter settlement reduce educational expenses by making uniforms and passing them to younger siblings, sharing textbooks among cousins or siblings who may be in the same classroom, or insisting that children earn their own money for expenses related to special projects or field trips. However expensive, education of the children is viewed as a very desirable and necessary goal. Again and again, the feeling is expressed that the children, once educated, will be able to move into the middle class and earn enough money to afford some urban pleasures and luxuries.

By 1974 a number of children born in the squatter settlements or who came as infants with their parents from the highlands were old enough to attend secondary school. The majority of those living in Ciudadela Chalaca and Dulanto attend a secondary school located in central Callao. As with their elementary school children, the parents of those attending secondary school are responsible for uniforms, texts, supplies, and the maintenance of the buildings. The cost of extracurricular activities such as sports participation and field trips also increases as children reach the secondary grades.

In 1969, when some of the children from migrant families were attending secondary school, a commonly expressed desire was for these students to attend a university or have post-secondary training. By 1974 a proportionately large number of those who had completed secondary school either were attending San Marcos National University or were taking post-secondary technical training at state-run institutions. A large percentage of secondary school graduates complained that the applications for admission to San Marcos far exceeded openings. For example, it took Hernán three years and three examinations before being accepted to study biology. After finishing secondary school, Carmen failed to be admitted to San Marcos for two years. She then traveled to her family's highland community to teach elementary school as a third-category teacher (one who has a high school diploma only) for one year. Then she persistently returned to Ciudadela Chalaca to study for the entrance examination for San Marcos to be given the following year.

LANGUAGE

One of the characteristics of urbanism in Peru is the use of Spanish rather than Quechua or Aymara. In the squatter settlement of Benavides, Mangin (1973:203) found the following languages in use among adults:

Spanish only	255
Quechua only	81

Spanish and Quechua	203
Spanish and Aymara	1
No information	21

Similar language use is found in Ciudadela Chalaca and Dulanto. A certain amount of ambivalence is expressed by many migrants regarding the speaking of Quechua. It is universally recognized that Spanish is the official language in Peru and also that Spanish is the language closely associated with an urbane and modern way of life. In contrast, the speaking of Quechua is symbolically associated with the isolated highland communities from which many migrants have come; Quechua is also associated with the low status from which many of the migrants have attempted to escape and from which they hope that their children will to some degree be disassociated. However, most of the adult migrants who speak both Spanish and Quechua view Quechua with nostalgia. In the squatter settlements, particularly when kin from the highlands make visits, Quechua is spoken with relish. A somewhat romanticized pride in provincial origins is beginning to be expressed by the residents of Ciudadela Chalaca and Dulanto. Likewise, the obvious gusto with which popular *huaynos* sung in Quechua are listened to on the radio and danced to at some festive occasions are indications of the continuing appreciation for Quechua.

The ambivalent feelings about language are reflected in the teaching of children in the squatter settlements. Most parents stress that it is necessary for their children to learn to speak Spanish well if they are to excel in the city. Most children who were born in the squatter settlements speak primarily Spanish; some also speak Quechua, and many more understand some Quechua but do not speak it.

CHANGES IN AGE COMPOSITION OF FAMILIES

The age composition in the squatter settlements presents a picture quite different from that found in the highland communities. A number of studies of rural-to-urban migration in Peru indicate that the great majority of migrants are between the ages of 19 and 28. For example, Matos (1966b:72), in his study of the squatter settlement Ciudad de Dios in 1955, found that only 4.7 percent of the population was over the age of 50 and that 48.6 percent of the population was under the age of 20. The Dirección Nacional de Estadística y Censos

(1968:8) found the following distribution of migrants' age of arrival
in Lima between 1956 and 1965:

under 14	5.9%
15-19	39.2%
20-24	19.9%
25-29	10.9%
30-34	6.3%
35-39	3.9%
40-49	5.8%
50 and up	8.1%

Both sexes are fairly equally represented among the migrants.
Martínez (1968:4) found among migrants the sex ratio was 54.3
percent men to 45.7 percent women. Matos (1968) found that women
were 48.4 percent of the squatter settlement population, while men
were 51.6 percent. Thus, through selective migration the makeup of
most squatter settlements consist of a young population composed
primarily of couples and young-to-teenaged children. Except for the
rare parent who came with the young couple, the oldest residents of
Ciudadela Chalaca and Dulanto who migrated to the city in the 1940s
and 1950s were nearing the age of 50 in 1974.

The desire to migrate in general is conditioned by a number of
factors, but the reasons why migration by the Peruvians is particularly
concentrated within a young age group is specific to this setting. In
the highlands the youths and newly married couples are often squeezed
out economically and given comparatively low status. The option of
migration to the city, particularly to those youths who see no opportunity for land ownership in the highlands, is often very attractive.
By the 1970s the migration of youths and young couples had become
an institutionalized means of coping with population excess in the
highlands and the desire for change and upward mobility among the
young people. The essential lack of persons over 50 years of age has
many implications for the character of the squatter settlements. The
young population is future-oriented and involved in building and con-
solidating an economic base as well as striving for upward mobility.
There is a dynamic sense of pioneering effort and youthful enthusiasm and striving.

In the squatter settlements grandparents are not present as they
are in the highlands to care for their grandchildren or tend to household tasks, thus freeing their adult daughters to work unhampered

outside the home. While many of the women in the squatter settlements do work, there is a strong sentiment that life would be much
easier were an adult consistently present to care for preschool children. To solve the problem, mothers generally take their infant children
to work with them, leaving the care of toddlers to older children who
also help tend to household chores. In contrast, many residents of
the squatter settlements commonly mention that their home villages
in the highlands are often almost devoid of young couples and laugh-
ingly indicate that only the old people have remained to watch over
the land.

Another change in family structure brought about by the rural-
to-urban migration is that in the squatter settlements the absolute
number of kin with whom each individual has contact or has the potential to mobilize alliances is smaller than in the highlands. For both
the individual remaining in the highlands and the migrant to the
coastal urban center, the full complement of kin is smaller than it
was in the period before the large-scale migrational movement began.
However, although the full complement of kin may not be present
in the coastal squatter settlements, a very large number of kin and
paisanos are nevertheless still present and even more accessible and
concentrated than they ever were in the highlands.

THE REMODELING PROGRAM

CHAPTER 2

In 1973 the government-sponsored remodeling of Ciudadela Chalaca took place. Ideally, the current houses in Ciudadela Chalaca were to be razed and replaced by uniform-sized lots in rectangular blocks, facing straight narrow streets. The residents of the area were then to be assigned lots on which they could build sturdy houses according to government-provided architectural plans once the plumbing and electrical services had been supplied. A central area for a soccer field and public facilities such as a meeting hall, marketplace, medical post, church, and park areas were planned.

Before the remodeling there was an official awareness among community members that uniform lots and streets wide enough for a car would eventually be necessary if the residents ever hoped to obtain official titles to their lots and if the community would ever be able to receive regularized community services such as water, electricity, and garbage pickup. However, many residents also realized that a modified residence pattern would mean a dispersal of the paisano residential groupings which had provided a great deal of physical and

In the background of this view of Sector A in Ciudadela
Chalaca in 1974 are public housing apartments.

psychological support for them during their initial years in the city.
The remodeling and subsequent relocation of some families presented a crisis period in which a decision among various options was
mandatory.

Five hundred families decided to stay in Ciudadela Chalaca and
were assigned new lots in a lottery. About 400 households that did
not immediately qualify for a lot because of their relatively short
residence in Ciudadela Chalaca and that did not elect to relocate in
Dulanto were settled in the areas ideally meant for eventual construction of community facilities. These families were termed excedente.
They hoped to eventually qualify for lots in other remodeled squatter
settlements. About 400 families chose to move to the new development

of Dulanto. Approximately 150 households moved out of the squatter settlement altogether, by purchasing a lot with money they had saved over the years, arranging for company housing through their employment, or moving in with kinsmen who lived outside the squatter settlement. Eligibility to remain in Ciudadela Chalaca or obtain a lot in Dulanto was officially based on three factors: length of residence in the squatter settlement, family composition, and "community spirit." However, many informal mechanisms, based primarily on the strength and influence of an individual's personal network, had some impact on the final decision as to which families qualified for lots.

On the day of the remodeling a fleet of bulldozers set to work razing the existing houses in Ciudadela Chalaca. Since many of the families had salvaged reusable building materials from their homes the work of the bulldozers was simplified. Five hundred lots were surveyed and marked with chalk, and families began to construct temporary houses to use until the plumbing and electrical services would be installed and construction could begin on their permanent homes.

Most families had known they would be moving for weeks and, once the remodeling began at one end of the squatter settlement, a general packing up was begun throughout. When their removal became imminent, families began to disassemble their houses and, packing their belongings into *tricycles* (carts propelled by bicycles), moved them to their new lots in Ciudadela Chalaca. Many families succeeded in moving large sections such as entire walls or roofs intact from their houses, which they then reassembled on the new lots. One resident said, "We worked without sleeping for two days and one night; and we worked hard, but we moved and built our house again in that time." The new lots were surveyed and measured and marked with white chalk lines, and metal stakes were pounded into the ground at the lot corners. As the remodeling progressed, large piles of rubble and debris began to accumulate throughout the squatter settlement. One resident remarked, "More dust and rats' nests were disturbed than we knew were here." Most households then proceeded to reconstruct their houses on their new lots over the next few weeks. When possible, siblings, or siblings and cousins, aided in the finishing of house construction with the mutual expectation of reciprocal aid in the construction of their houses.

During the relocation process, many of the families who moved from Ciudadela Chalaca to Dulanto removed large portions of their houses to use in the construction of their temporary houses. One of the favorite and most amusing stories of the relocation was recounted by

Eusabio many times at social functions in Dulanto. He told of bringing the entire front of his house, complete with the door and window, from Ciudadela Chalaca to Dulanto on his tricycle. His two nephews walked along to steady it. To compound the problem, it was a very windy day, and the housefront kept blowing off. When they reached Dulanto, they propped up the housefront and used the front door as access to their empty lot where they camped for two weeks until building a temporary house of esteras.

EFFECTS OF THE REMODELING AND RELOCATION PROCESS

During the relocation process from Ciudadela Chalaca to Dulanto, SINAMOS assigned each block in both settlements an identifying letter. The new residents of each block were expected to organize as a block unit by electing three delegates to attend bi-weekly community meetings. In many other respects, the block was designated as the official unit of organization. For the residents of each block, many of whom were located on lots which were back to back and who were rarely paisanos or kin, identification and organization by block is in direct contrast to the traditional inward-looking pattern of paisano clusters which was found in Ciudadela Chalaca prior to the remodeling.

After the remodeling in Ciudadela Chalaca the houses were primarily constructed of esteras and wood, and the interiors were very similar to those described previously. The medical post, dining hall, and church had been removed. Nine of the fourteen water caños remained after the remodeling and only one of the soccer fields remained. The meeting hall had been razed, but a smaller temporary one was built. The police station, the school, and the marketplace remained. Although all of the electric lines were torn down, during the remodeling the residents quickly re-formed their electric cooperatives and reestablished electric service. By 1974 the population was conservatively estimated at 6,300. Persistent rumors indicated that an additional number of recent migrants had clandestinely joined their kinsmen in the excedente section.

The relocation program in 1973 represented a drastic change for almost all of the residents of Ciudadela Chalaca (Figs. 2.1–2.4). The residential clustering of paisanos from the environs of Huirahuacho in Apurimac, for example, originally included 84 households and approximately 540 individuals in a characteristic pattern. A semi-secluded open space of about 120 square feet in the center of the cluster contained a water spigot which was the focal point of much daytime activity. The houses faced inward toward this plaza area. The arrangement of passageways to the area discouraged those who did not live there or have immediate business there from entering. After the remodeling program the previously clustered Huirahuacho group was dispersed. About half of the original households remained in Ciudadela Chalaca, while the others were relocated throughout a four-block area in Dulanto. The plaza and the clustering of paisanos were eliminated. Some of the newly formed conjugal families that had previously lived in the household of one set of parents managed during the relocation to obtain a temporary lot in the excedente area, with the hope of eventually being assigned a lot elsewhere.

During and following the remodeling the ambivalence regarding the changes was evident. Many families joyously awaited the day when the remains of the old houses would be razed by tractors and new lots assigned. It was said that Helsomina was so overjoyed at the prospect of her family finally owning its own lot that she wept and knelt to embrace her assigned space. Pascual, who in 1974 had a house facing on a street, commented, "Where we were before, back at the end of that little alley, there was no air and we were always sick. Here there is much more fresh air and sunshine and we are hardly ever sick." In Ciudadela Chalaca the prospect of one day building a substantial house and having access to some of the amenities of urban services as well as the positive symbolic value given to home owner-ship was a powerful impetus for acceptance of the remodeling.

In contrast, a number of negative comments centered on the dispersion of the paisano and sibling groupings. Susana, who had spent 41 of her 45 years in Ciudadela Chalaca, her family being one of the first to settle in the area, was very distressed with the remodeling. Her eldest son said, "She cried for three days when she saw that the lot we got was so far [one block] from everyone else." Fernandina, a member of the paisano grouping from Apurimac, many of whom went to Dulanto, said after the remodeling, "We're all alone and sad. . . . It used to be so happy here with everyone around."

In Dulanto, the lottery system utilized to determine lot assignment further dispersed kin and paisanos. Some siblings thus dispersed both in Ciudadela Chalaca and Dulanto attempted to rectify the situation through trading of lots. However, others feared to tamper in any way with the lots which they had been assigned by SINAMOS for fear of losing rights to any lot. Also the time and expense involved in officially effecting a change was almost always prohibitive. After the relocation a great deal of effort on the part of the residents of

Figure 2.1 Ciudadela Chalaca prior to the 1973 remodeling ordered by the government. About 12,000
people lived in the nine-hectare area.

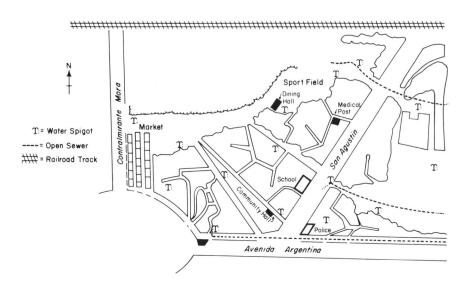

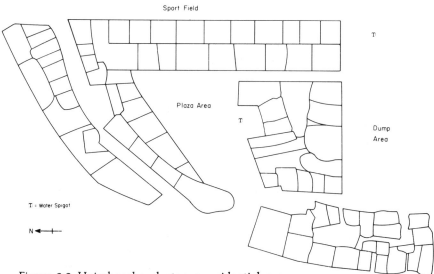

Figure 2.2 Huirahuacho cluster, a residential group
of 84 paisano households in Ciudadela Chalaca,
before the 1973 remodeling. The houses faced the
semi-secluded plaza.

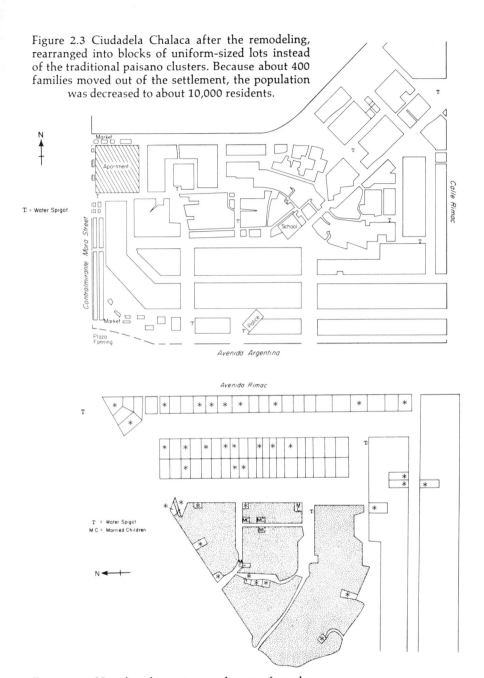

Figure 2.3 Ciudadela Chalaca after the remodeling, rearranged into blocks of uniform-sized lots instead of the traditional paisano clusters. Because about 400 families moved out of the settlement, the population was decreased to about 10,000 residents.

N

T = Water Spigot

Market

Apartment

Market

Plaza
Fanning

School

Police

Avenida Argentina

Calle Rimac

Contralmirante Mora Street

Avenida Rimac

T = Water Spigot
M.C. = Married Children

N

Figure 2.4 Huirahuacho paisano cluster after the remodeling. The asterisks indicate original Huira-huacho households; the rest of the paisano families moved to the new settlement of Dulanto. The shaded areas indicate the blocks of households classified as excedentes, to eventually be relocated.

both Ciudadela Chalaca and Dulanto was placed on maintaining close contact between kin and paisanos. Short visits take place from home to home and during the daily marketing, while on Sundays visiting and socializing between Ciudadela Chalaca and Dulanto occurs on a large scale. However, the extra effort which must go into maintaining these previously convenient relationships is an activity which the residents see as diverting precious time and energy from providing for basic subsistence needs or the construction of their new houses.

The most extreme cases of isolation after the remodeling are found among the families who through their jobs or individual effort arranged to purchase homes in housing developments removed from Ciudadela Chalaca. Ava, at 21, had lived her entire life in Ciudadela Chalaca at the time of the remodeling. When she, her parents and five siblings moved into a home obtained through her father's company, Ava said:

> I really miss my group of friends in Ciudadela Chalaca. We used to lean against the cement wall of the market place in the evenings and talk and laugh together. Now that Ciudadela Chalaca is all changed, the whole group has split up. At first when we moved here, I felt so unsure of myself. I just didn't feel right about doing anything. In Ciudadela Chalaca, your friends or your enemies, somehow they all gave you support. But here it's just not the same. In Ciudadela Chalaca, you could just walk outside and there was everything you might want to buy or do. Not here.

Before the remodeling, complaints regarding life in the squatter settlements centered around the lack of modern amenities such as electricity, sewers, and fresh water, and not on the population density. After the remodeling, positive comments focused on the opportunity to soon build a solid house with electricity, water, and sewage. Most complaints of the remodeling process concerned the dispersion of the paisano and kin groupings due to the changes in the migrant initiated settlement pattern.

By October 1974, 14 months after the initial resettlement of residents on uniform lots in Ciudadela Chalaca, SINAMOS still had not initiated work on the water, sewage, and electrical systems, nor given the residents the building plans which were to be followed in house construction. Additionally, during remodeling the medical post, soccer fields, open sewers and a number of the communal water spigots were removed and not replaced, leaving fewer public facilities. Also, rumors that the land occupied by Ciudadela Chalaca might be confiscated and the residents moved to yet another area, added an additional note of uncertainty to the potential for eventual land ownership and the construction of permanent houses.

One of the largest investments in terms of money and labor to every migrant family that comes to Lima is the eventual purchase or construction of a house. Various optional methods exist for the construction of a family home. However, these options are always circumscribed by considerations of insecurity of land title and scarcity of funds for material and for labor.

The problem of insecurity of land title is reflected in the degree of permanence of building materials which are invested in the construction. Where insecurity is greatest, building materials are less expensive and less permanent. In 1964, houses in Ciudadela Chalaca were constructed primarily of scrap lumber, much of which had been scavenged throughout the city. Some few houses were constructed of esteras, and esteras were most often utilized in the construction of second-story sleeping rooms. By 1969, the insecurity of ownership of the lots precluded construction with more expensive and permanent materials. Although many families had accumulated some expensive sets of bedroom or living room furnishings and appliances such as television sets and refrigerators, the house construction remained primarily that of scrap lumber. By 1969 many had constructed second-story sleeping rooms of scrap lumber also and esteras were rarely seen in the squatter settlement. By 1974, with the division of the settlement into lots but with security of ownership remaining unconfirmed, the residents still lived in temporary housing, as reflected in the use of wood and esteras for construction. Ideally, at the time that construction is permitted in Ciudadela Chalaca, it will be carried out with concrete and bricks according to specifications indicated on the house plans which will be provided by SINAMOS.

In Dulanto, a similar evolution of construction materials occurred, though at a much more rapid pace due to the relative security of land title which existed at the time that the relocation to Dulanto took place. Most families initially constructed houses of esteras or readily assembled wood which were utilized as temporary shelters until construction could be begun with more permanent materials. One year later in April 1974, very few of these temporary shelters existed without at least the foundations of the permanent structure in construction. Many families by October 1974 had built some of the exterior brick walls of their houses and lived inside these.

The second consideration, that of scarcity of funds for materials and labor, was resolved through two strategies: the plan to work hard and save a consistent portion of the earnings for construction costs and the mobilization of one's network of kin or non-kin alliances for aid in obtaining materials and labor. The general high value among the migrants from the highlands placed on hard work and saving money for future goals is an important factor in their ability to construct temporary houses rapidly and to begin construction on permanent dwellings once title to a lot is secured. When direct cash for materials and perhaps construction laborers is insufficient, the strategy of mobilization of the reciprocal aid network of both kin and non-kin is activated.

THE DEVELOPMENT OF DULANTO

There are 1,136 lots in Dulanto. Four of these blocks contain the residents of a small squatter settlement called José Olaya that originally occupied the northeast corner of what is now Dulanto. The 400 households which moved from Ciudadela Chalaca represent about one third of the incoming families; the remainder came from other remodeled squatter settlements in the metropolitan Lima area.

The area of Dulanto was formerly agricultural land for truck farming. Similar farms still occupy the land located on the north side of the Rimac River, across from Dulanto. In the late 1960s this area was purchased as a potential commercial housing development. Lots were surveyed, a well was dug, and major sewer and water pipes were laid. The installation of street lamps was begun. However, the sale of lots was held up because Dulanto is directly in the landing pattern of the international airport. The area stood dormant for a few years until it was sold to the Peruvian government as a relocation area.

In 1974 Dulanto had water piped to each house for two hours a day, a public elementary school, a small preschool, a community hall, a small market, a soccer field, and a number of open spaces where parks were planned (Fig. 2.5). By September of 1974 the street lights had become functional and a number of families had set up electric cooperatives. Houses were in all stages of construction. Some families still lived in the temporary structure of esteras and wood, but most families had the surrounding wall and a portion of the brick first floor constructed, while a few families had completed construction of two stories.

All of the families who moved to Dulanto had to pay at least 2,000 *soles* for the right to settle (2,800 soles is the monthly income of a man who earns the minimum wage). This sum represents the

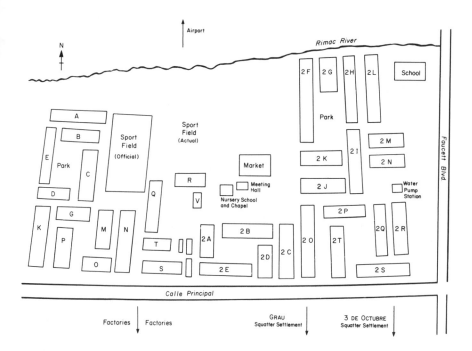

Figure 2.5 The government-sponsored settlement of Dulanto, a relocation area for about 1,200 families from remodeled squatter settlements. Families were assigned lots, which were arranged in blocks, by lottery.

initial payment for the lot, the total cost of which is 20,000 soles paid over a three-year period. The agreement is handled by SINAMOS and specifies that title will be transferred to the resident family at the completion of the total payment. The initial payment entitled each family to become a legal "possessor," live on the lot, and begin house construction. The monthly payments for the lot, as well as a charge of 150 soles a month for water and public lighting, were begun in October 1974.

The building and remodeling of squatter settlements into working-class neighborhoods is a process which is visibly occurring within the Lima metropolitan area. In squatter settlements in which residents feel confident that they will be allowed to remain in the area and to eventually obtain legal title to property, there is a relatively rapid

House construction in Dulanto.

transformation from the first temporary structures to solidly built houses. The settlement of Carmen de la Legua, for example, in 1965 was considered a barriada within the district known as Reynoso. By 1969 Carmen de la Legua was known in Ciudadela Chalaca, located about two miles distant, as one of the most "progressive" squatter settlements in Callao. By 1974 its transformation into an urban barrio was almost complete — paved roads, uniform lots, water and electrical services, urban-style houses constructed with permanent materials, and a central plaza around which stood municipal buildings, a movie theater, and a church all were established. Being within only a few blocks of Dulanto, Carmen de la Legua stood in 1974 as a visible example of what "we can all do if we work together," as one resident of Dulanto observed.

For those families living in Dulanto various methods exist to obtain materials and mobilize labor for house construction. The most common strategies include one or a combination of the following: loans from employers, credit cooperatives among residents, reciprocal labor exchange among kin and paisanos, and block associations for labor exchange. A very few families living in Dulanto, but none who had come from Ciudadela Chalaca, received cash to be spent for housing directly from the company for which they work in lieu of their purchasing one of the company-financed homes in a nearby, commercially operated housing tract. In Dulanto five households received funds which were sufficient for them to purchase all of the materials necessary for their house construction and to pay laborers to construct their houses in a short period of time. A small number of families who had received funds from their places of employment also completed the first stories of their homes through the use of paid laborers. A few other families who had saved sufficient funds or who were able to sell land or stock which they owned in the highlands were also able to build complete houses soon after moving to Dulanto. However, this manner of house construction was unusual enough to be considered by the other residents of Dulanto as somewhat deviant behavior and the object of some envy and mistrust. As one resident said, "People like that really should not be here. This community is for families who build their own houses."

The most common method of obtaining funds for house construction is to join one of the various savings cooperatives which allow for access to large supplies of cash with which to buy materials. In one form of savings cooperative, called a *pandero*, each family puts from 150 to 200 soles per week into a general fund. Then a weekly lottery is held to determine which of the member families will take the entire pot for that week, a strategy which avoids the high interest rates requested by banks for loans. In Dulanto there are also some cooperatives based on skills such as carpentry or plumbing in which reciprocal exchanges take place. Generally these cooperatives, as with most voluntary associations, are organized along kinship and paisano lines.

The credit cooperatives are a partial solution to the problem of raising funds sufficient for the purchase of materials in wholesale lots. However, the problem of sufficient labor still exists, since much of the building requires that a number of individuals work simultaneously during certain phases, such as during the mixing and pouring of cement for the foundation. Usually near kin, most notably siblings, are recruited for reciprocal labor exchanges during the construction period. When possible each family works alone on house construction, calling on kin for aid in specific tasks. Much of the construction work is carried out on weekends and during holidays.

By 1974 very few of the families who were building their houses through only the reciprocal aid of kin and paisanos had reached the stage of pouring the roof. The general consensus is that within five years most houses should be finished. In the meantime the families live in various combinations of temporary shelters and half-completed houses. For many this combination is considered far superior to the cramped housing that they may have had for years in a squatter settlement such as Ciudadela Chalaca. For other residents, who are in the minority and who may have had rather substantial houses in Ciudadela Chalaca or other squatter settlements, the partially completed housing of Dulanto represents an inconvenience. Their close proximity to the airport is another disadvantage. A number of times each hour all conversation must cease as the planes roar overhead. Additionally, governmental intervention at many junctures, for example in providing only four house plans from which the residents must choose, inhibits initiative and the creative solution to problems which was so prominently a part of Ciudadela Chalaca prior to the remodeling. However, the complaints regarding Dulanto are outweighed by the pervasive sense of positive striving and feeling of accomplishment expressed by the residents.

ECONOMIC STRATEGIES

CHAPTER 3

Tanto tienes
Tanto vales.

What you have
Is what you're worth.

En la casa del herrero, cuchillo de palo.

In the house of the iron worker, knife of bark.

Economic motivations are fundamental to migrational movements in Latin American areas. In Ciudadela Chalaca migrants often speak of the nearly hopeless economic situation in their highland villages. The variation in sources of income found in Ciudadela Chalaca and Dulanto is vast, and the ingenuity with which individuals often find or create and later maintain sources of income for themselves is notable.

An investigation carried out in 1969 by the Oficina Nacional de Estadística y Censos (1969:29) found the following employment percentages in the squatter settlement El Agustino, located near the central market district of Lima:

Office work	6.7%
Labor	1.8%
Personal services	52.7%
Domestic work	5.7%
Vending with pushcarts	33.1%

In Ciudadela Chalaca and Dulanto most of those who work outside the area have jobs in factories, on the docks, or as market vendors. However, this type of gross generalization fails to give a true picture of sources of income.

In Ciudadela Chalaca and Dulanto there is a wide range of income among the residents; incomes also vary seasonally. For example, most of those who work in factories earn the minimum wage of 80 soles per day for women or 100 soles per day for men. A man who works six days a week is paid for seven, thus earning 2,800 soles per month (about $80.00 U.S. as of 1974). More may be earned through overtime work or a variety of part-time jobs. A more experienced factory worker may earn up to 16,000 soles per month, and some fishermen in the past have earned up to 30,000 soles per month in the peak season. In a general sense the economic status of the inhabitants of Ciudadela Chalaca and Dulanto is similar to that found by Millones (1975:61) in the Pueblo Joven of Huerta Perdida, in which 69.45 percent of the respondents claimed an income of less than 7,000 soles per month. Judged on the standard criteria of an eight- or nine-hour work day and a fixed remuneration, however, the income of many household units is deceptive. While some individuals do earn a steady income working a set number of hours daily, most residents make their livings through a much more complex and varied manipulation of *cachuelas,* or odd jobs, of exchanges of labor for goods, or of exchanges of labor for labor. Most households recognize the necessity of maintaining a varied and flexible repertoire of these techniques. The economic pattern is one based on diversity, manipulation of resources and hard work, with the goal of amassing capital. Arrangements for providing for income are an almost constant point of concern and a frequent topic of conversation in Ciudadela Chalaca and Dulanto. Additionally, the seasonality of many sources of income requires frequent shifts in income strategies.

Previous economic investigations regarding types of employment and earnings of migrants or others living in squatter settlements have often overlooked a number of vital factors, thus tending to produce inadequate and often grossly incorrect data. Methodologically, the use of income of the "head of household" for determining household economic level, as Uzzell (1972:302ff), Valdivia (1970:48ff), and others have done, is inappropriate for gaining a realistic picture of sources and amounts of income in the squatter settlements. Here a mature woman is admired for being a *buena trabajadora* (good worker) more often than for being attractive, and all members of the household are expected to contribute as much as possible to the economic well-being of the family unit. Another methodological oversight found in many economic studies of squatter settlements is the emphasis placed on employment that fits into preconceived or traditional occupational categories. Individuals whose sources of income are not within traditional categories are often lumped as "unemployed," "underemployed," or "miscellaneous," which designations fail to give a true picture of sources of income. Some studies consider only employment in which there is direct monetary remuneration, overlooking exchanges of labor for goods, exchanges of labor for labor, or the fringe benefits derived from a job. These fringe benefits include such cases as the taxi driver who may make personal use of his taxi or the tacit agreement between factory workers and management that a small amount of goods will either officially or unofficially be resold by the workers. For example, one man who lives in Dulanto and works in a factory which makes electrical plugs keeps a box of about fifty of these plugs in his house which he then sells to his neighbors at a discount. In most accounts of employment and income of residents of squatter settlements there is no adequate consideration of the seasonal nature of some types of work. Other aspects of income are changes in income due to age and experience. Another methodological shortcoming is the conception of yearly or even monthly income, which is not congruent with the way in which most households in the squatter settlements view their incomes. While many household units would be hard pressed to give an exact figure of monetary income for a given calendar year, almost all households would, if they cared to, at any given time be able to supply a detailed account of the current state of their economic resources, including the balance of reciprocity in social relationships. Uzzell (1972:257) feels that some male informants underestimate their actual income when in the presence of their wives in order to conceal from their spouses the exact amount of their income. While some individuals may be motivated by such considerations in discussing their economic resources, there exists a much more widespread and encompassing Andean cultural pattern of a general reluctance to discuss one's resources, particularly to an outside investigator who is too easily identified with tax collectors or other municipal employees.

Most individuals living in the squatter settlements of Lima have a studied reluctance to answer formal questions, particularly those dealing with resources and family members and their activities. The primary motivation for consistent underestimations of resources is that prestige and power and control of resources are viewed as essentially interwoven phenomena. An exact knowledge of one's material resources and the extent of one's network of interpersonal influence could be used to undermine one's position of prestige and power within the community. There is a realistic fear that others, chiefly through envy or desire for personal gain, might strip one of power if the exact extent and nature of this power was understood. As power is conceived of in terms of wealth in material aspects and in personal relationships, an attempt is made to avoid discussing these topics except in a nonspecific and inexact manner.

The tendency to underestimate the exact nature of resources is due to a desire both to avoid invidious comparison and to maintain the secrecy of one's resources. In the highlands, where there exist asymmetrical power relationships between the mestizos and the Indians and between the urban and the rural dweller (and where there formerly existed such a relationship between the hacendados and the peasants), the less advantaged conceal certain feelings, activities, and resources. This pattern has been developed to a fine art as a basic and often realistic survival technique in relationships with any individual who may in some way threaten these resources, who may exert power over one, or who is not "one of us." In the squatter settlements of Lima a similar attitude is maintained regarding government employees, the police, census-takers, or potential thieves or con artists who may ask questions regarding resources and whose motives are not clear.

As a result of the high value which is placed on diligence, however, there is a tendency in some instances to overestimate resources in order to demonstrate one's cleverness and hard-working nature. In the squatter settlements appliances such as television sets and refrigerators are often displayed prominently as evidence of the family's ability to work and save money. The yearly cycle of fiestas and the parties commemorating rites of passage such as baptisms and weddings are often ostentatious demonstrations of wealth.

Although a number of women in the market sell potatoes side by side, each vendor has her "clients," that is, shoppers who always return to buy from her.

THE MARKETPLACE

The marketplace is in many respects a focal point in the daily concerns of each family. In the 1970s, 290 to 310 separate vendors were active in the small market in Ciudadela Chalaca. In Dulanto there is a similar market with 36 vendors. In Ciudadela Chalaca some of the shoppers include residents of a nearby working-class neighborhood and a government-owned apartment complex. In both Ciudadela Chalaca and Dulanto there are more vendors present on Saturday and Sunday. The vendors who are active only during the weekends generally have full-time jobs during the week. Compared to the week-day market, the Sunday market presents a festive air with greater representation of novelty items such as clothing, records (often with demonstrations played on a record player and amplified with speakers), plastic containers, and specialty foods such as *picarones* (sweet fried bread).

Variation is found in the supply of certain commodities. For example, meat is often regulated by the government, which maintains certain days on which beef, lamb, and pork is to be sold; fowl and fish, which are considered less desirable, are sold daily. During 1974 the recurring scarcity of certain products, such as canned milk and rice, was sometimes suspected by the residents of Ciudadela Chalaca and Dulanto to be the result of speculative hoarding by wholesalers. Seasonal variation is also found in the availability of fruits, most of which are transported from the tropical eastern side of the Andes. Over a period of months variation in who sells and what he sells also occurs. A woman may sell *moliente* (a warm herb drink) during the cold months and then switch to picarones during the summer. Another may sell the crocheted baby hats that she makes, but only when her supply warrants. Some vendors sell for only a short time, while others, particularly those who possess a permanent stall, remain in the same spot selling the same type of merchandise for years.

In Ciudadela Chalaca and Dulanto each household purchases food daily. The daily trip to the market provides both economic and social functions. Generally, the women do the shopping since it is they who prepare the meals. Purchase of foodstuffs and preparation of food represent a large portion of the female head of the household's concerns. The morning trip to the market, in which food is selected for the entire household's consumption, generally lasts about an hour and is carried out efficiently, yet enough time is allowed for many brief greetings and short exchanges of information between kin and paisanos and between vendors and buyers. The market represents a focal setting for communication, for sizing up the available products, for commiserating on rising prices, and for exchanging quick bits of information with intimates. Bargaining is minimal. Buyers generally frequent the same vendors, expecting lower prices in exchange for their continuing patronage.

For most residents of Ciudadela Chalaca, commercial transactions of one type or another are an important aspect of one's selfconception of being a productive member of society. Evaluations of status in terms of money or reciprocal labor exchange are not far behind a resident's appreciation of a vendor's potatoes, a kinsman's new clothes, or a paisano's television. The ebb and flow of interpersonal relationships as well as the evaluation of one's standing in the social hierarchy are measured and often maintained on a basis of economic criteria and interchange. A great value is placed on economic transactions and in following the ups and downs of prices, cultivating patron-client relationships, and seeking to improvise ingenious and often multiple commercial transactions. Many of these economic concerns center on the marketplace.

Traditionally in the highlands of Peru the majority of market vendors are women. This pattern of small-scale, commercial middlemen (or women, in this case) is also found in the squatter settlements. Most of the market women from Ciudadela Chalaca and Dulanto relish the role as well as the opportunity to be actively engaged in commercial activities. Those women who are not currently vending in the market are nevertheless the household members who carry out or at least oversee the bulk of family expenditures, those for food and clothing. Until 1973 very few residents of Ciudadela Chalaca paid rent, and thus the largest daily expense was for food. After the relocation those families who moved to Dulanto began to spend a large proportion of their incomes for house construction, while those remaining in Ciudadela Chalaca began saving for the time when they could begin permanent construction. Thus women more than men are highly attuned to the fluctuations of supply and of price in the marketplace and to managing household finances.

ARTISANS

In Ciudadela Chalaca and Dulanto there are many artisans involved in the repair and creation of articles. There is a fluctuating number of tailors, some of whom work full time and others of whom work part time when not employed elsewhere. All tailors are men and each generally specializes in one type of article of clothing, such as men's wool pants, men's sport coats (which many men use as overcoats on chill winter mornings), or women's coats and suits. Most tailors work in their homes, although some work in clothing factories. Women who are seamstresses work in clothing assembly shops outside the squatter settlement. A number of individuals work in shoe repair within Ciudadela Chalaca and Dulanto. There are those who repair electrical appliances, such as televisions, radios, or other household equipment, and those who repair kerosene stoves, the most common source of cooking heat.

A number of common services are also supplied within the boundaries of Ciudadela Chalaca and Dulanto. Haircuts for men and chil-

In Dulanto a barber offers movable service on Sundays. He brings his equipment, a chair, and comic books for his clients to read.

dren are taken care of by family members or housefront barber shops scattered throughout the settlement. In 1974 in Ciudadela Chalaca there were three young women who had set up small beauty salons in their homes. A number of women in Ciudadela Chalaca and Dulanto have signs posted by their doors indicating that for a small fee they will administer an injection. Some of these practitioners have taken a short course from the local public health nurse. A few individuals, primarily women, also cure the traditional illnesses of *susto* (soul-loss illness often caused by a bad dream) and *ojo* (illness primarily in children which is the result of a "look" by a person who has the power to cause sickness). Generally, however, the treatments of these illnesses, which fall outside the domain of European medicine, are carried out in a less openly commercial manner. Three women in Ciudadela Chalaca also work as *parteras* (midwives), attending women who have their babies at home.

SMALL COMMERCIAL ACTIVITIES

Some families in Ciudadela Chalaca and Dulanto prepare food for boarders. Because of the strong feelings of trust which must pervade a situation in which food is given and received, boarders are generally relatives or at least paisanos. Consistently eating *en la calle* — that is, buying food from the street vendors — is considered a disagreeable and often unhealthful practice. It is thought to be much preferable to eat in the security of the home of relatives, where the food is prepared with the care and in the manner of one's wife or mother.

Families which own refrigerators often charge kin or paisanos a small fee for food storage. Those families which own television sets may also choose to allow neighbors to pay two soles in order to watch special shows. The most popular are the daily afternoon soap operas, or *novelas*, which are watched by the women, and the sports shows, particularly the soccer matches, watched by the men on the weekends. The novelas are most commonly produced in Peru, Mexico, or Venezuela and reflect an idealized version of middle- and upper-class values; they not only function as entertainment but also provide knowledge of middle- and upper-class behavior patterns, much of which is of use to migrants in dealing with urban situations. A large number of families also raise guinea pigs, rabbits, or ducks for their own consumption and for sale. These animals, particularly the guinea pigs and ducks, are considered foods for festive occasions.

FACTORY EMPLOYMENT

The Avenida Argentina is the main industrial area of Callao. Both Ciudadela Chalaca and Dulanto are within walking distance of a number of factories and within busing distance of others. Bus fare is 2½ soles. The proximity of this large number of potential sources of employment is one of the positive attributes of both Ciudadela Chalaca and Dulanto; for residents in some other settlements, located on the far periphery of the metropolitan area, one-and-a-half-hour commuting trips by bus are often necessary. Most employment is found in textile factories, shoe factories, fish canneries, fish-meal factories, beer-bottling factories, factories where small appliances are assembled, and the slaughterhouse. Most of the residents of the squatter settlements who are employed at one of these factories are paid the minimum wage of 100 soles for men (or 700 soles per six-day working week) and 80 soles for women per day. These wages must be viewed in terms of the purchasing power that they represent: in 1974 a kilo of potatoes at Ciudadela Chalaca cost 6½ soles, and a poor cut of beef cost 70 soles per kilo. Between January 1973 and January 1974 the price of cereals in Peru rose 37.12 percent, the price of vegetables 43 percent. In Lima between 1966 and 1973 general consumer prices rose 191.98 percent (Oficina Nacional de Estadística y Censos 1974d:3,13). Obviously the residents of the squatter settlements, like other Peruvians, are fighting against climbing inflation. In a family of two adults and four children, one person who earns the minimum daily wage would just barely be able to cover expenses for food. However, the low minimum wage, when coupled with the wide range of cachuelas in which most households engage, provides income ranging from just enough to subsist, to surplus with which to purchase appliances, send children to private schools, or build a house. The factory jobs are considered desirable since they provide some stability of income compared to the fluctuations of cachuelas. Some factory workers with special skills earn well. However, many men and women, particularly those who are young, are maintained at the minimum wage and without the fringe benefits of social security and union membership by being dismissed from a job just before completing the 90-day probation period, after which they would have been considered full-status employees. For example, 23-year-old Alejandro tells of having been dismissed from his sixteenth factory job in a cannery, again shortly before the 90-day, minimum-wage period ended. However, many individuals in the squatter settlements who have found positions which they like and at which they are skilled have managed to maintain their positions for years, qualifying for higher and higher salaries.

Certain types of employment in factories allow employees the opportunity to obtain both clandestinely and officially some of the products produced there. Those who work at the slaughterhouse are considered particularly fortunate as they are often able to obtain enough discount meat for their extended families or for resale. Because of their access to meat, a very high-prestige resource, the slaughterhouse workers can excel as hosts at fiestas, in which meat dishes are an indicator of generosity. In a more formalized fashion one of the large shoe factories issues ten-percent discount cards to its employees for seconds.

If an employee is in a union, the dues subtracted from his pay average about 28 soles weekly. The unions function primarily as political and social organizations and may also sponsor the factory soccer team. In 1974 employees of one shoe factory on the Avenida Argentina went on a 40-day strike in demand of higher wages and other benefits. The act of refusing to work was seen by some in the squatter settlement as foolish and by others as courageous, since the unions do not provide striking members with compensation. In this case a small pay increase was obtained when sympathizing union members at other factories struck for two days. For most of the migrants who live in the squatter settlements, union membership, philosophy, and tactics represent new ideas. After the successful strike, discussions in Ciudadela Chalaca and Dulanto of the events were mixtures of expressions of satisfaction and incredulous elation that workers could actually force the management to increase wages.

Social security benefits, although they exist theoretically, have little actual effect for individuals living in the squatter settlements. In Peru employees are divided into two distinct categories, roughly corresponding to "blue-collar" workers and "white-collar" workers. Factory and related workers are classified as *obreros*, or blue collar, while those who have desk jobs or who are government employees are generally considered *empleados*, or white collar. Those who work as domestic servants, as vendors in small stalls, or who combine a variety of cachuelas escape formal inclusion in either category. It is significant to note that employees, even those who have desirable factory jobs, are not able to depend on union or social security benefits in times of crisis, nor is there a functioning social welfare system that reaches the residents of the squatter settlements. In the squatter settlements an individual turns to his kin and paisanos for aid during times of crisis. A number of individuals living in Ciudadela Chalaca and Dulanto are employed by the anchovy fishing industry (Pesca Peru) and the mining industry (Mina Peru), two industries recently expropriated by the government. Jobs with the Mina Peru are considered by those in Ciudadela Chalaca and Dulanto as particularly well-paying and stable; additionally, they offer opportunities for skilled training, advancement, and some fringe benefits. Some families living in Ciudadela Chalaca in 1969 were by 1974 living outside the squatter settlement in company-owned, modest yet modern houses which they had begun purchasing through long-term, company loans. Likewise, Pesca Peru was arranging for company-financed housing in 1974.

Since Callao is the principal port of Peru, a number of jobs are available as porters in the loading and unloading of freight vessels and in the warehouses. Some of the jobs are considered good, as the pay is somewhat more than the minimum wage.

Some men living in Ciudadela Chalaca and Dulanto drive taxis or *colectivos*, cars with standard straight runs along busy thoroughfares. Ownership is often shared by two or three men, most often brothers, who make maximum use of the car by driving it in shifts.

DOMESTIC WORK

A number of individuals, particularly women, work as domestic servants in neighborhoods often quite distant from the squatter settlement. This type of job is typically held by young unmarried girls, particularly those who have recently arrived from the highlands, have no other skills, and lack the independence which maturity offers. Although governmental controls have technically improved working conditions for domestic servants, this type of employment is characterized by long hours, very low pay, heavy work, and often lack of respect. Most of the young women who work as live-in domestics generally only have Sunday afternoon off, at which time they come to stay with their parents or other relatives in the squatter settlements. Many matronly women in their late thirties and forties now living with their families in Ciudadela Chalaca tell of their first years in the city when they worked as domestic servants. Most of the reminiscences are bitter tales and focus on harsh treatment. However, some remembered patrons who were "fine people" who paid for their servants' books and uniforms and allowed them to attend elementary or secondary schools. Ernestina, who was approaching her mid-forties, recalled vividly the three years she worked as a live-in domestic when she was a teenager. She recounted with unconcealed mirth and ribald pleasure how she was dismissed after she taught the son of the family for whom she worked to say a typical highland sexual insult in Quechua instead of "Good morning, professor," as the son had requested. When he unknowingly greeted his university professor with this scandalous phrase in Quechua, the son was punished and Ernestina was fired. She told of laughing uproariously as she rode the bus all the way back to her kinsmen's squatter settlement. Some of the women living in Ciudadela Chalaca and Dulanto who previously worked as domestic servants became pregnant through a relationship with a member of the household in which they worked. Some ceased working at that time; others continued to work, and their children became integrated into the patron family household in a "poor cousin" status.

In Ciudadela Chalaca a few mature women, particularly widows, work as part-time domestics carrying out washing, a very strenuous and heavy job by the Peruvian method of boiling and scrubbing the clothing. These women work in the neighborhoods within walking distance of Ciudadela Chalaca. In Dulanto the opportunity does not exist for part-time domestic work since the community is somewhat isolated from contact with middle-class neighborhoods where washing might be done. Most women who have worked as domestics indicate that this type of work is generally very disagreeable and should be taken only as a last resort; they certainly hope that their children never have to be thus employed.

PROSTITUTION AND THIEVING

Living in Ciudadela Chalaca and Dulanto are a number of individuals who work in occupations which, from the viewpoint of the migrants from the highlands, are considered quite undesirable. These two occupations, prostitution and professional thievery, form a type of subculture which is primarily composed of criollos who have lived all of their lives in an urban setting and who interact very little on a social level with the migrants living in Ciudadela Chalaca or Dulanto. There is even distinct residential segregation within the squatter settlements between the highland migrants and those families which specialize in such undesirable occupations.

Approximately four blocks from the east side of Ciudadela Chalaca, between shipyards and surrounded by factory walls, is a well-known landmark of Callao, El Trocadero. This brothel, according to all informants, is believed to be the largest in the Lima-Callao area. It has an active work force of 300 women, as well as bouncers, ticket-sellers, maintenance crews, and the personnel who run the numerous restaurants attached to the establishment. The employees of El Trocadero are almost exclusively criollos. The building itself is hangar-like with two stories of small, stall-like rooms. Tickets are sold at the door in three price ranges. Most of the women who live in Ciudadela Chalaca and work at El Trocadero are employed in the section in which tickets are the least expensive (40 soles each). Contact with each client lasts from five to thirty minutes. The women receive a set wage in addition to a small percentage of the ticket tales and on occasion a tip from customers. The women who work in El Trocadero report that this occupation is not without its appeal, although generally it is seen as physically exhausting and boring work. One resident of Ciudadela Chalaca commented that it was work to which she could turn to feed her children whenever her husband was in prison. She considered it much more desirable than being a domestic servant or a vendor of vegetables in the market, low-status jobs she judged more suitable for the migrants from the highlands. On the other hand, the migrants who live in Ciudadela Chalaca and Dulanto generally view El Trocadero as *bárbaro* (ridiculous). The women comment that they would much prefer hard honest work in which they would be respected, while men comment that to pay for sex, a commodity which can be obtained for free, is an absurd waste of hard-earned money.

One young man made the following analogy. In his highland community the market is an open-air one, in which the buyers know all of the vendors. One takes time when making a purchase to enquire about their families and discuss the comparative merits of their merchandise. Purchases are made in a friendly, slow-paced fashion between individuals who have relationships of long standing. In contrast, in some neighborhoods in Lima and Callao there are supermarkets where one just rushes in and grabs what he wants. "But somehow it is just not the same and the food does not taste as good." He commented that El Trocadero is like these urban supermarkets.

Ciudadela Chalaca, another squatter settlement about three blocks to the north, and an adjacent working-class neighborhood are known in popular folklore in Lima and Callao as focal areas of criminal activity. This belief is not without some foundation since the squatter settlements provide the advantages of anonymity and lack of police investigation to those families engaged in robbery as a profession. Like prostitutes, professional thieves are almost exclusively non-migrants. Some professional thieves in Ciudadela Chalaca and Dulanto are well known in Peru and hold celebrity status in the underworld. One individual, who is now "retired" and living on the proceeds from his past, even served as the model for a swashbuckling villain in a continuing comic-book series. Most thieves carry out their professional activities outside the squatter settlements, especially in the middle-class districts. If they were to practice their profession within the boundary of the squatter settlement, the social ostracism that might follow would deprive them of the safe cover that the squatter settlement provides.

The relationship between the highland migrants and those coastal people who are engaged in illegal activities is primarily characterized by tacit avoidance and mutual disrespect. The reputation of the criollos' fierceness and skilled use of knives is matched by the sheer numbers and cohesive nature of the highlanders' kin and paisano groups. This point is illustrated by an incident, one of the few approaching physical violence that I observed, in which two women, one the wife of a well-known underworld figure and one a member of a large paisano highland group, began to argue over usage of the public outdoor spigots around which clothes are washed. Both women were in their mid-thirties, matrons, mothers of some consequence, and known as women of strong character who would not let themselves be dominated. The argument reached a crescendo as insults led to shouts. The coastal woman's husband, whose skill with the knife was well known, appeared, as did more than forty male and female relatives of the highland woman. The confrontation reached a standoff when the coastal man shouted threats to use his knife and insults to the effect that "You all are a bunch of sheep," while the mute and stern array of highlanders stood firmly with folded arms. Both parties backed away and the women saw to it that they used the spigot at different times. One highland woman in the kin group commented later that this confrontation was a prime example of the necessity of kin solidarity and one positive aspect of having many kin. However, this incident was a very rare instance in which a confrontation nearly became violent, the more usual pattern being avoidance of conflict through avoidance of contact.

Not all illegal activity is carried out by criollos or zambos. However, within the squatter settlement there are definite tendencies in employment and income sources along lines of ethnicity and place of birth. For example, market vending, petty commercialism, and domestic labor are almost exclusively in the hands of the highland migrants. Incomes related to prostitution and robbery are almost exclusively the domain of criollos. Fishing tends to be associated with criollos, while factory work is predominantly held by highlanders. The two groups share a residential area and many facilities, but they do not share belief systems or values regarding what is one's appropriate and honorable work.

DEPENDENT ADULTS

Work in some form or another is almost universal among the adult population. However, some very few adults are completely dependent on others: these include the completely physically disabled and the insane. The chronically infirm are cared for, though sometimes grudgingly and in a perfunctory manner, by relatives. Because of the distribution of ages within the squatter settlements, there are proportionately very few elderly and infirm who must be cared for by kin.

The insane are sometimes confined within the homes of their kin; if they have no kin present or willing to care for them, they live on the streets, often near the marketplaces in the squatter settlements. Those who live on the streets depend on obtaining discarded clothing and food. Their often bizarre and sometimes aggressive behavior is treated with avoidance and constraint. These destitute insane are frequently referred to pityingly as "poor creatures."

EMPLOYMENT FUTURE OF YOUTH

In the 1970s in Ciudadela Chalaca members of the first generation of children born in the squatter settlements were just beginning to enter the job market. They had often had the opportunity to obtain much more education than their parents and were entering a variety of fields of employment. Those young men who have completed primary or secondary school and who are in their late teens generally find employment in the factories or as taxi drivers. This employment is often obtained through a relative's connections. Some young women who have taken technical courses in high school join the job market as secretaries. In 1974 two young women were students in a nearby state-run nursing school. One of the eight teachers in the elementary school in Ciudadela Chalaca spent his childhood and youth there. Another young woman recently received a teaching credential and began teaching elementary school in a nearby district of Lima. What the employment picture will be in Ciudadela Chalaca and Dulanto in the future when the increased education of this younger generation has been felt extensively is still a moot question.

JULIO AND HELSOMINA

The household of Julio and Helsomina provides an example of the wide range of economic strategies employed by the migrant families. In 1969 Julio and Helsomina lived with their six children in Ciudadela Chalaca. They had migrated from the highland department of Ancash when first married fourteen years before. In 1969 Julio had a steady job in a belt factory for which he was paid slightly more than the minimum wage. After work and on Sundays he intermittently

Julio, a tailor who specializes in men's trousers, works in his home
in the evenings and on Sundays, as do many other artisans.

worked as a tailor, making men's pants to order. Above the door to
their house was a large wooden sign indicating that they sold kerosene.
They kept a large drum of kerosene which they then sold in small
portions to neighbors who brought their own containers. Since the
majority of households cook with kerosene it is considered a basic
commodity. The entire family, but especially the children, were careful
to pick up any tin cans or scrap metal that they found by the street. The
metal was stored at the rear of the house until enough was gathered
to sell at a factory near Julio's work.

Helsomina had at one time sold vegetables in the local market,
but as her family became larger, she found this type of job impossible.
On occasion her first cousin, whose husband worked in a textile fac-

tory, was able to obtain small woolen scraps of textile. Then both women worked together for a few hours each afternoon to ravel the mill ends, tie them together, and wind them into balls. Some of this undulated wool was sold on consignment at the stall of a cousin in the local market, and the rest was saved for the family needs.

After an earthquake in the late 1960s Julio and Helsomina, with the aid of two young nephews who were living with them at the time, were able to salvage from the debris of destroyed buildings in the residential districts of Callao a large number of fired bricks and other miscellaneous building materials. Stacking the bricks without mortar, they were able to replace the wooden front wall to their house. In the back room of their house they formed a stockpile of the remaining bricks and other building materials that they then used in the network of reciprocal exchange among relatives. They sold some to non-kin whenever the demand presented itself. They also kept five to ten guinea pigs in their kitchen and three chickens on their roof. When their stock increased beyond the family needs, they sold the surplus. On three-day holiday weekends and during the longer holidays Helsomina made *chicha*, a traditional highland fermented maize drink, which she then sold to paisanos who came to their house in order to drink and play *zappo*, a game of skill in which a weight is tossed in numbered holes in a specially designed box. In 1969 Julio and Helsomina began installment payments on a black-and-white television set. Neighbors who came to watch the popular afternoon soap opera *Simplemente María* or the weekend sports events paid two soles per program. About five women watched the daily soap opera.

In 1974, five years later, the family had changed some of its economic strategies, but the fundamental style of diversity remained. They had obtained a lot in Dulanto and by October 1974 had begun construction of their permanent house. In the one and a half years since moving to Dulanto and before beginning their permanent construction, they lived in a temporary three-room house that in general style closely resembled their house in Ciudadela Chalaca. Julio continued his job at the belt factory, but his salary had only increased a small amount, hardly keeping up with the inflation that had occurred in the past five years. He also continued to work intermittently as a tailor in his home. The family no longer sold kerosene, indicating that it was too much of a fire hazard. However, the front room of their wooden house served as a small general store in which they sold soft drinks, rice, beans, spaghetti, and canned milk. They also sold bottled beer instead of chicha now that they lived only a few blocks from a beer factory and could pick up the cases of beer and return the empty bottles on the tricycle that Helsomina had once used when she sold vegetables in the market. As their new home in Dulanto was farther from the crowded streets adjacent to Ciudadela Chalaca, there was less opportunity to collect tin, so they had discontinued this practice. The cousin who previously had had access to the mill ends no longer was able to attain them. After moving from Ciudadela Chalaca, the family sold the remainder of the scavenged building supplies but kept the bricks for house construction in Dulanto. They no longer raised guinea pigs as before but did have a narrow corral running the length of their lot in which they had three ducks, two chickens, two sheep, and a small goat. Again, surplus animal products not used by the family were sold. The sheep yielded enough wool for Helsomina to spin it into yarn in the traditional highland manner, dye it, and knit it into sweaters for the children. On long weekends and holidays male kin and neighbors often gathered to play zappo in the lot in front of their house in Dulanto. Large quantities of bottled beer were then purchased on these occasions from their store. Neighbors continued to pay two soles to watch the daily soap opera and weekend sports events. Although proportionately more families had televisions in 1974 than in 1969, approximately the same number of women came to watch the daily soap opera. By 1974 Julio and Helsomina had also begun payments on a refrigerator. Besides using it themselves, they stored items in it for neighbors, who paid a small amount for this service. The profit obtained from the television and refrigerator earned slightly more than the monthly membership in the electric cooperative to which Julio and Helsomina belonged. By 1974 their oldest daughter was attending high school and learning secretarial skills. The family had purchased a small portable typewriter for her on which she typed occasional formal business letters or petitions required by governmental offices for neighbors for a small fee. The eldest son, who was studying electronics in high school, looked forward to soon opening a radio and small-appliance repair shop in their home.

VALUES

CHAPTER 4

A number of fundamental values that are shared by the migrants living in Ciudadela Chalaca and in Dulanto form an interlocking system that serves as both a rationale and a motivational force for decisions for action. The values held by the migrants help to explain why migration itself is regarded as positive and why goals of survival in the city and of upward mobility are tenable.

PROGRESS

Among the migrants the concept of progress, which includes implications of modernization, industrialization, urbanization, growth, and construction, is viewed positively. Modern urban centers, efficient industrial complexes, or individuals who are technically well trained are referred to as *muy adelantado*, that is, moving ahead or progressing rapidly. An individual, particularly a politician within either the local community council or at the national level, may be complimented for exhibiting characteristics of a *progresista,* of being very progressive. Conversely, rural areas and traditional modes of living and of economic production, although frequently referred to with nostalgia, are often considered *atrasado,* or very backward. Migrants frequently lament that a particular squatter settlement will never "progress" or indeed that Peru itself will not "progress." Urban centers are viewed in a positive light as areas where there is *movimiento,* or activity and excitement, while the rural highland communities are often referred to as *triste,* or sad and lonely.

Progress is viewed as moving away from something negative, in this case away from life in the highlands, which is remembered in terms of scarcity of food, illness without relief, severe climate, and tremendously hard and wearing work with very little compensation. Progress is also seen as moving toward the positive ideal embodied in urban living, exemplified by plentiful food, good health, productive work, and adequate pay. The act of migration from a rural to an urban setting represents to most migrants their power to effect sweeping and what they consider positive changes in their lives.

The migrants are thus able to view themselves as progressing according to their own criteria and dealing with change in terms of an ideal model of progress. By their standards, a great improvement has occurred in their lives since moving to the city. For example, once in Ciudadela Chalaca early in the morning a group of women waiting at the spigot, buckets in hand, began to comment on the comparative merits of rural and urban life. One woman grumbled at the bother involved in waiting her turn for use of the communal spigot. A number of the other women present adamantly protested, reminding her that in the highlands one must often walk long distances and carry water over steep terrain, while here in the city one only needs to step outside the door and wait.

Much of the Peruvian government's planning as reflected in the public media is focused on progress, as in, for example, the changes in the official designations for squatter settlements. By the mid-1960s squatter settlements were referred to both in the media and by the residents as *barriadas,* a word that intensifies the term *barrio,* or district. However, many official documents (such as Ley Orgánica de Barrios Marginales #13517) employed the term *barrios marginales,* or marginal districts. Also, by this time there were both technical and popular distinctions among *barriadas,* the inner-city *tugurios* (slums), and *correlones* (clusters of small, one-story apartments often arranged around an open passageway). As time went on, the term *barriada* gathered numerous negative connotations, particularly when used synonymously with terms for slum or in government agencies in which there was some desire for community development and change. However, among the migrants in the squatter settlements a certain sense of identification and at times sense of pride was associated with their homes in the barriadas. After 1968, when the government became controlled by a military junta, *barriada* was replaced officially by *pueblo joven* (young town), a term with implications of a community in the process of development and improvement. By 1974, although squatter settlements were officially still designated as *pueblos jovenes,* many residents continued to call them *barriadas.* An additional official twist was evident when families from Ciudadela Chalaca were relocated in Dulanto, which was referred to officially as an *urbanización popular* (a people's housing development). In actuality Dulanto followed much of the major developmental sequence found in many squatter settlements, especially those established through government sponsorship or mass invasion.

At the individual level, residents of the squatter settlements see themselves involved not only in change in the form of urbanization and modernization but also in change in the form of mobility. In the squatter settlements the concept of upward mobility is closely interwoven with the ideals of progress and change. The initial move from a rural area into the national capital is seen as a very large step toward upward mobility. Upward mobility is viewed primarily in terms of attaining the material goods associated with middle-class urban Peruvians. These are a house in the city; appliances such as a television, stove, and refrigerator; and stylish clothing. Typical highland goals of an abundance of food and economic resources that allow one to sponsor large festive events are also seen as desirable. In spite of the rigidity of the Peruvian social hierarchy, at the lowest levels, the opportunities for upward change and the enthusiasm for making this change are abundant. Change is seen as a daily potential to be seized when the opportunity arises and worked for with persistence.

The migrants feel fairly sure that the future will be an improvement, if not for themselves then at least for their children. Much of this change is the result of explicit goal-directed efforts and careful planning. For example, between 1964 and 1969 in Ciudadela Chalaca houses generally became more and more sturdily constructed and more second stories were added. By 1974 the families who had relocated from Ciudadela Chalaca to Dulanto were living in incipient two-story, brick dwellings in contrast to the homes of esteras and scrap lumber from which they had come.

HARD WORK AND SAVING MONEY

In sharp contrast to a generalization often quoted in regard to Latin American mestizo populations, "fate" does not play a particularly vital role in the migrants' perception of events. Fate may be the ultimate, though not often evoked, explanation for an unexpected death or a hopeless life situation; however, the degree to which one is willing to work is a much more common basis for explaining one's situation in life. Individuals from the highlands view industriousness as a necessity for survival as well as a positive attribute. Working hard is considered the correct and moral way to participate in society. A wife commonly praises her husband because he works a great deal. Likewise, a married woman is rarely complimented on her physical beauty, but her husband often indicates with considerable pride that his wife is an excellent woman because she is "a very diligent and industrious worker." For example, it is the general consensus of kin and paisanos as well as of Enrique himself that when he married Isabel, who is ten years his senior, not particularly attractive, and has a cantankerous personality, he chose a fine woman because she "is a very efficient and skilled worker and has her own stall in the market."

Among married women in the squatter settlements the most common complaint regarding their husbands is that they are not working as they should or earning enough money to raise the children. Another common criticism is that even if the husband works hard, he spends too much money on weekends drinking beer. Likewise, a common complaint of husbands is that their wives are neglectful of their duties and spend too much time watching daytime soap operas on the television. Unmarried teenagers who are the children of highland migrants indicated that a spouse should ideally be attractive physically, know how to dance and dress well, and be *bien preparada* — well educated and prepared to work well.

An individual who is able-bodied but who does not work hard enough is viewed as immoral and is often referred to as a *desgraciada* (disgraceful one) or a *sinvergüenza* (shameless one). These two words are reserved primarily for the rare migrant who is slothful or for the urban criollos, who follow a more leisure-oriented ethos and a more relaxed lifestyle than the migrants from the highlands. In contrast to other parts of Latin America, where the term *sinvergüenza* carries strong implications of sexual immorality, within the Peruvian squatter settlements this negative label implies a failure to fulfill economic obligations.

A shoe repairman works in his outdoor stall in Ciudadela Chalaca.

A common theme in the literature dealing with Latin America is the hispanic ethos, the result of upper-class Iberian influence, in which there is a disdain for working with one's hands or hard physical labor in which one perspires. The residents of the squatter settlements, by whom the merit of a job is judged primarily in terms of the remuneration obtained, make very little attempt to avoid a job that entails hard physical labor or working with one's hands. While a job that is *suave* (soft and easy in a physical sense) is appreciated, almost any job is acceptable regardless of the extent of physical labor, as long as financial returns are adequate. In fact, work with one's hands in the squatter settlements is viewed by many with considerable pride. Satisfaction is obtained through production as an expression of industriousness. The shoe-repair man with a small stall in one of the side streets of Ciudadela Chalaca exhibits with obvious pride his various techniques for repairing shoes. Fernandina, who kneads large and heavy quantities of dough and then dexterously forms sweet fried breads at the marketplace, remarks that her muscles feel good after she has been kneading dough all morning and that she enjoys the stares of passersby in the market as she forms the circular *picarones* and drops them in oil. Felice expresses obvious pride as he describes in the presence of his family how, after fifteen years of working at one textile factory, he is able to run eight weaving machines simultaneously, a skill which entails not only considerable experience and dexterity but also the necessity of being on his feet and moving rapidly between the machines throughout the day. Most individuals, both men and women, take this same pride in their work and their ability to be productive and economically solvent. This feeling stems at least partially from the value that stresses the necessity for hard work, both as a means to economic survival and upward mobility and as a desirable end in itself.

Many of the jobs carried out by the residents of Ciudadela Chalaca and Dulanto entail long or irregular hours. Jobs related to commerce and marketing generally begin before dawn. When the opportunity arises, factory employees work overtime. Some men may work at two full-time jobs for short periods of time in order to meet extraordinary economic demands. The long hours of daily work are partially a function of the low wages and buying power of those living in the squatter settlements. However, they are also the result of the social approval given to work and to productivity itself. Married women, most of whom have a number of children and extensive food preparation and household chores to complete, often not only contribute money to the family income but also enhance their own prestige through work, most commonly by vending in the market or from a housefront store.

During the work week very little time is generally spent in leisure activities; by nine or ten in the evening most of the alleyways and streets of Ciudadela Chalaca and Dulanto are quiet and the houses are darkened as families prepare for bed. Between five o'clock and six-thirty in the morning the squatter settlements are alive and bustling with activity as workers prepare to leave for the day. The early morning radio stations blast forth the popular huaynos in both Spanish and Quechua as families prepare and eat breakfast. During the week most adults rarely sleep more than seven or eight hours each night; they sleep considerably less during the weekends when nighttime socializing commonly occurs.

Children are taught the importance of working hard and, by five years of age, many are an integral part of the family effort, aiding in child care of younger siblings, carrying water, washing clothing, running errands, or helping parents with their stalls at the marketplace or in housefront stores. Children are also exhorted by their parents to study hard in school so that they will excel and become bien preparados for their future employment. Although parents work hard to provide educational opportunities for their children and take pride and interest in their schoolwork, they also make many demands on their children in the form of household responsibilities. This training is in anticipation of adulthood, in which each individual has economic responsibilities that are intricately tied to reciprocal obligations to kin. Both men and women are expected to excel at work as well as to actively maintain numerous alliances.

The effort exerted by school-age children has in many cases provided positive results. For example, in 1964 Lucilla, the oldest of eight children, was doing well in her second year of high school at age fourteen and wanted to be a schoolteacher. Her younger brother Lucho wanted to go to college. In 1969 Lucilla was studying at a normal school, and in 1971 she received a standard teaching degree. By 1974 she had been a schoolteacher for three years, her brother Lucho was studying electronics, and a younger sister who had attempted to enter the San Marcos university but who had failed the entrance test was working as a teacher's aide. Three younger siblings expressed a desire to follow their older siblings' examples. This family is not extraordinary in the educational attainment of their children. The social impact of the remarkable disparity between the educational level of the parental generation and that of the children born or raised in the squatter settlements will become increasingly evident in the future. In 1974, however, the ongoing educational achievements of the youth were an indication of the strength and motivating force of values stressing hard and persistent work and the positive value attached to change and upward mobility.

The desire for education is not limited to the youth. Many adults attend literacy and elementary school classes at night at the public school in Ciudadela Chalaca as well as in private homes. Often the recently earned primary school diploma of an adult member of the household is framed and displayed next to those of the children of the family.

The few elderly residents of Ciudadela Chalaca and Dulanto, as well as those suffering from extreme illnesses, continue to work, though often at a slowed pace; no time arrives when one feels socially justified in completely ceasing to participate in carrying out family obligations.

The elderly work not only through a need for survival but also because respect is gained through a demonstrated ability to work diligently. They care for young children or help in the preparation of food in order to maintain a minimal level of family participation. Like Luisa, who lives with her son and his family and who is in her late seventies and almost blind, some elderly carry out small-scale commercial enterprises. Luisa sits during most of the day next to a small box at the front door. Here she displays candy, fruit, and individually wrapped cookies that she sells to the children who live nearby. Her net earnings are small, but she earns dividends of respect for her desire to be an economically viable member of her family.

Interwoven with the positive sanction given to industriousness is the equal importance given to the ability to accumulate resources. It is believed that resources are obtained through diligent work and the manipulation of interpersonal relationships to create advantageous options. The money thus obtained must ideally be put aside for expenses. Primary priority is given to construction of a home once title to a lot is obtained, educational needs of the children, sponsorship of fiestas, and purchase of major appliances.

In Ciudadela Chalaca and Dulanto almost every family, no matter how close to the bare survival line it may be, manages to place a portion of earnings aside. Residents carefully hide this money in their houses, on their persons, or in some instances it is deposited at credit unions or banks. The exact amount of the savings or even their very existence is kept a strictly guarded secret to avoid envy and to conceal the extent and nature of resources controlled in order to manipulate circumstances to one's advantage. There is usually a sense of ample opportunity to acquire resources, but the precise details of one's strategies must be guarded as family "trade secrets."

The ability of many of the families to save considerable sums of money over a period of years was particularly evident in 1974, thirteen months after the first household had moved to Dulanto. By then a number of the families which had previously lived in Ciudadela Chalaca had completed partial construction of their houses, the materials for which often cost up to 100,000 soles, much more than could have been saved during the preceding year. Another example of planning for large future expenditures can be seen in expensive wedding or baptism ceremonies and in the sponsorship of fiestas. For example, Antonia and Merino began living together at her family's home in 1972. By July of 1973 adequate resources had been accumulated by both families for a civil ceremony and party. In April of 1974 the considerably more elaborate and expensive church wedding and party was carried out. Three of the guests shrewdly calculated expenditures to be between 18,000 and 20,000 soles, while the mother of the bride estimated that each family had spent 30,000 soles for the religious wedding. This sum represents more than ten months' income for an individual earning the minimum wage in factory work. These are expenses made possible through the long-term accumulation of both capital and reciprocal obligations that balance out in favor of the host of the event.

The migrant residents of Ciudadela Chalaca and Dulanto find themselves in direct contrast to the criollo population, whom they characterize as never planning ahead but merely enjoying the more ephemeral pleasures of life, such as faddish clothing, expensive culinary delicacies, and gambling. Conversely, the criollos characterize highlanders as somber hard-workers who take no pleasure in living.

BEING WITH PEOPLE

In both Ciudadela Chalaca and Dulanto being with others is felt to be vital to one's happiness. Solitude is seldom needed or desired. It is viewed as a natural characteristic of human nature to desire to interact daily with a large number of individuals, and there is a general press toward reaching agreement and acting with unity. The social ideal is for each individual to participate fully in multiple relationships, fulfilling many obligations and becoming the recipient of many reciprocal benefits. Power, prestige, and ultimately the basic pleasures of life, as well as one's survival, are thought of in terms of interaction with others. There are a number of common expressions regarding the need to belong to a family unit, the need to be near those who love one, the need for a man and a woman to live with one another and share the responsibility of raising children, and the need for siblings to share one another's concerns. These are ideals, yet they provide motivation for behavior.

In Ciudadela Chalaca in 1969 the population density was equal to about 553 persons per acre. Close contact with others was not difficult to arrange. In 1974, after the majority of lots had been assigned in the remodeling, the density was decreased to approximately 460 persons per acre. In Dulanto, with its relatively wide streets and open community areas, the density is approximately 250 persons per acre. To the migrant residents the density, although at times inconvenient, provides the overwhelming advantage of accessibility to kin, paisanos, and many others. A number of social mechanisms are present to reduce tension that might otherwise arise in a high-density living situation.

The archetypal characterizations of slums as "swarming" and "teeming" have often been applied to squatter settlements. From the perspective of an outsider there may also be a generalized tendency to make an *a priori* assumption that a dense population is undesirable in all respects. In Ciudadela Chalaca, before the irregularity of lot size and unavailability of urban amenities became considerations, crowding *per se* was not viewed as particularly burdensome or as a focal point of concern. The remodeling was seen by the residents not primarily as an opportunity to decrease the density of the population but rather as an opportunity to obtain legal title to land through the regularization of lot size.

One of the commonly expressed advantages of residing in the city, even in a squatter settlement, in contrast to the rural highland areas is the presence of a large number of people. Rosa made the typical comment that, "here in the city, it is so fine because one is never alone. In the highlands it is very lonely and sad, but here I am so close to many more of my paisanos." The sentiment is often expressed that an individual with many kin is fortunate, secure, and in many respects wealthy, whereas one who has few kin considers himself unfortunate and poor. Even those families that consider themselves thus without many kin may, at important occasions such as a wedding celebration, be able to invite two or three hundred kin from the squatter settlement.

In Ciudadela Chalaca the only negative comments regarding the population density were expressed in regard to the inability of some recently married young couples to establish their own households. The criollos at times spoke disparagingly of the highlanders, referring to them as *carneros* (sheep) because they "move together in herds," or as *cuyes* (guinea pigs) not only because many migrants raise guinea pigs in their homes but also because the criollos view the migrant families as procreating at the same rapid pace as guinea pigs.

One of the most difficult aspects of fieldwork for me in the squatter settlements was what I considered the extreme population density. I was in close physical contact with other people, usually many other people, twenty-four hours a day. My desire for privacy seemed peculiar to most of the residents of the squatter settlements. To work on my field notes, for example, I waited until the houses in which I stayed in Ciudadela Chalaca and Dulanto were relatively empty in mid-morning. However, as soon as I took my typewriter into an empty room or corner, an adult would follow me or more commonly would send a young child to sit with me so I "would not feel lonely all alone."

Fundamental to the migrant's ability to cope daily with the dense population is the value that stresses that interaction with people is desirable. One who is alone is considered to be sad and lonely. During life crises, particularly childbirth, weddings, illness, and death, there is a gathering of kin and paisanos. For example, soon after the birth of a baby, kin begin to arrive to see the baby and to "accompany" the mother for the next few days; otherwise it is believed the mother may become sad. Likewise, the success of a wedding celebration or a wake is measured at least partially in terms of the number of guests who "made everyone feel happy." During illness, including the time preceding death, it is believed to be extremely important for the bedridden to be accompanied so as not to be "alone and sad." Solitude is never particularly sought after, while the necessity for steady contact with people is felt to be vital.

In addition to the desire for social interaction, there are a number of social mechanisms that help to accommodate the dense population and allow the residents to maintain generally amiable and often mutually supporting relationships. When relationships are not amiable, there is at least a generalized avoidance of overt conflict. Hatred or dislike is countered by a sense of tolerance or avoidance and ultimately with the knowledge that there is no immediate escape from life in the squatter settlements and the complex web of relationships which this life entails: thus one *must* get along with others. In spite of the lack of privacy and the necessity for sharing scarce community facilities such as water, residency within the squatter settlements is viewed as a positive step toward access to permanent title to land, and thus much tolerance and restraint must be practiced in order to maintain this advantage.

Much of the interaction between individuals is low-keyed. Because of the numerous relationships in which each person is involved, any one relationship is less intense than might be the case if such a wide range of actors was not present. Additionally, the large kin networks and the paisano groupings act as a buffer and deterrent to overt hostility and violence both within and between the groups. For example, although the average number of individuals within each household is greater than six, family members rarely intrude on one another in a physical way. Loud or annoying personal habits are avoided and care is taken to be nonintrusive with others. Although many households have televisions or radios, these are generally played softly so as not to be an annoyance. Although some houses are separated by just a thin wall of esteras or a combination of esteras and scrap lumber, care is taken to assure privacy and avoid habitually making loud noises. There are socially acceptable exceptions to the avoidance of loud noises such as parties or celebrations. Belligerence occasionally erupts during celebrations in which large amounts of chicha or beer are consumed, but family members are quick to restrain or stand between individuals who might come to blows. Underlying all of these efforts to be considerate of others is a belief that people should get along with one another and that each person is responsible for the harmony of the group.

Within the squatter settlements animosity, envy, and other forms of dislike certainly flourish. However, conflict resolution is such that overt physical aggression rarely occurs and conflict is held at a tolerably low level, especially considering the density of population. Within the household, squabbling among children is not tolerated and rarely presents itself as a problem because siblings from a very early age are taught the necessity of sharing with one another and getting along with others in the family. Among adults within the family, disagreements are usually settled through avoidance and only rarely reach physical violence. While some people who engage in crimes live in Ciudadela Chalaca, they work outside the squatter settlement and respect those who live there. For example, Bertha told of the day that she and her teenage sister dressed up and went to downtown Lima to windowshop. While walking along the street, she felt someone trying to snatch her purse. She swung around to face the thief, only to see that he was an acquaintance of hers who also lived in Ciudadela Chalaca. They both laughed and he profusely apologized, saying that he had not recognized her. He offered to walk the girls to their bus, but they refused, telling him, "Not with a sinvergüenza like you who tries to rob someone from his own barrio!" The incident became a standing joke among the youth of Ciudadela Chalaca who did not let the thief easily forget his mistake.

A confrontation involving an overflowed sewer occurred in 1969. Two different paisano groups shared a small open space in which they threw their rubbish. When an open sewer began to overflow onto the field, rumors flew from each group that the other was responsible for throwing rubbish into the sewer and plugging it. In the afternoon of the first day, as a stinking pool began to grow in the field, a number of women from each paisano group confronted one another and began to argue loudly across the pool of fetid water. Without exception, the women stood with their arms folded across their chests in a pose of strength as they argued. That evening two women, one from each group, who happened to be comadres, conferred and decided to take up a collection to pay someone to unplug the sewer. The next morning each woman took a collection in her paisano group; they put the money together, and by evening the sewer had been cleared and the pool had begun to dry. The men in both paisano groups had intentionally stayed out of the controversy and within a few days relations were again amiable between the two groups.

A degree of tolerance is also demonstrated in regard to the acceptance of the few insane individuals or other extreme social misfits who live within the squatter settlement. Individuals who occasionally drink to stupefaction or those who are habitually drunk are treated with good-natured tolerance.

Another mechanism through which smooth social interaction is usually carried out is that of reciprocity. Reciprocity in all relationships is also directly related to the commonly held value that one should be industrious. One who is not a hard worker, and thus is not able to uphold his or her reciprocal obligations, is excluded from the net of reciprocal ties considered vital to survival and prestige. The establishment of reciprocal ties is viewed as a positive accomplishment even if one is initially placed in the negative position of being the giver who may go into debt. An ongoing reciprocal relationship or exchange represents an expansion of the net of influence and an opportunity for continued interaction and possibly upward mobility.

Reciprocity is fundamental to social relationships. The goods and services exchanged in the squatter settlements include information, training, job assistance, money, sharing of facilities, moral and emotional support, food, invitations to festive occasions, and the hospitality offered to visiting kin. Food, for example, is offered to guests at all social functions, including weddings, birthday parties for adults, baptisms, wakes, parents' receptions at the primary school, and informal visits between families. The food served at a wedding is the aspect of the celebration most often remembered and discussed in detail and is also most often the target of critical comment after the celebration has long passed. The ritualized offering of beer which occurs at most social events is another occasion when food figures in reciprocal interaction. "We don't know them well, as we have not sat down to eat together," is a common statement indicating the degree of friendship.

Small gifts of food, whether consisting of hot milk and coffee served in the home or a bag of potatoes placed nonchalantly in another's hands, are considered the gifts of hospitality, the initial gestures upon which reciprocal alliances are founded and perhaps eventually maintained. The giving of food symbolizes a generosity and a desire to replenish another individual, while the taking and consumption of food represents an acceptance of the donor's intention as well as a trust and appreciation of the wholesomeness of the food offered.

It is customary for kin visiting from the highlands to bring with them large sacks filled with the produce of the land to distribute as gifts, delicacies which for the most part are difficult to obtain in the city. These include potatoes, *quinoa* (grain), the flat coarse highland bread, goat cheese, chickens, and guinea pigs. These foods are then distributed to urban kin, who savor these small symbolic remembrances of their homelands. When residents of the squatter settlements make trips to their highland villages, it is their obligation to take bags of used clothing for their side of the reciprocal exchange and on their return to bring home some bags of food for their kin who had to remain on the coast. The use of food as the basis for initiating and continuing reciprocal relationships is an example of one mechanism for getting along with others.

PART TWO

The Social Network

Young nuclear family in Ciudadela Chalaca.

KINSHIP

CHAPTER 5

The clustering by paisano groups is not discernible within the squatter settlements upon first contact. Only when some knowledge of the inhabitants of each dwelling is obtained and mapping is carried out do patterns become clear. On the ground the lack of obvious boundaries between different paisano groupings adds to the initial impression of a chaotic settlement pattern. The use of nonstandard and greatly varied construction materials contributes to the appearance of confusion and disorganization. This impression may have influenced the generalized statements that one finds (for example, in Fried 1959; Martínez 1968; Mejía Valera 1966; Patch 1957) in which the apparent disorganization of residential patterns is extended to include social and psychological aspects of the squatter settlement.

The almost complete lack of literature dealing with topics of kinship within the squatter settlements is an indication of the lingering viewpoint among social scientists that kin relationships are attenuated or absent in an urban setting. One of the common assumptions in many studies of urbanization is that families and therefore kin affiliations are "fragmented." As a result, as Adams (1968:1) notes, there has typically been little interest in urban kinship among social scientists, and much of what is known derives from the study of kinship in "Western society." Thus Young and Willmott (1957:12) could write in all honesty of their "surprise to discover that the wider family, far from having disappeared, was still very much alive in the middle of London." The meager amount of interest and investigation of kinship in almost all studies of urban migrants (the few exceptions for Latin America include Butterworth 1962; Kemper 1974a; Lomnitz 1977; Mangin 1970; Peattie 1970; and Safa 1974) has been accompanied by an attempt to stress a shift in the city from some of the previously rural kin functions to voluntary associations or governmental or private social service institutions.

In Ciudadela Chalaca and Dulanto, however, private or governmental social service institutions and voluntary associations play a relatively minor role compared to that of kin and paisanos. As mentioned previously, the social services offered through both governmental and private institutions are not highly effective in serving or even reaching the vast populations of migrants living in the multitude of squatter settlements throughout the metropolitan Lima area. Numerous writers (for example, Doughty [1970] and Mangin [1955a]) have stressed the role that voluntary associations play during the adaptation process in Lima. Many voluntary associations exist and are often led or sponsored by an individual who is not a member of the community. The frequent lack of success in the organization and maintenance of these voluntary associations (in which the members are not linked through kin or alliance networks) may be one of the characteristics that have led some to label the social organization within the squatter settlement as "disorganized" or "breaking down." The proliferation of individual networks, however, continues to function within the squatter settlement milieu according to the migrants' own plan.

From the viewpoint of each migrant, the use of many other forms of relationships, such as those found in extensive kindreds or those formed through alliances such as marriage, is the most expedient manner of insuring trust and reciprocity. A look at the composition of voluntary associations such as the soccer teams or the paisano clubs in Ciudadela Chalaca and Dulanto reveals that the individual participants are generally linked through numerous and overlapping kin and alliance networks. It is these networks, and not membership in voluntary associations *per se*, that provide the fundamental fabric of social interaction. The attitude of many migrants is that one may join a voluntary association in order to solve a problem or attain a common goal, but the unity of the group is an expression of kin solidarity or previously initiated networks of alliances and is not primarily the result of group membership.

THE KINDRED

An ego-based kindred with a strong sibling tie is the fundamental form of organization which is found among the migrant residents of Ciudadela Chalaca and Dulanto. The kinship system in the squatter settlements is bilateral with a degree of patrilateral emphasis and is similar in many respects to the basic pattern reported for the Andean highlands (Carter [1977]; Custred [1977]; Lambert [1977]; Mayer [1977]; and Webster [1977]).

Linkage

One pertinent characteristic of a kindred, in contrast to a lineal orientation, is that the members of ego's kindred are related to ego through a connecting relative and not through a shared ancestor (Goodenough 1970:41ff). For example, while carrying out fieldwork in the squatter settlements of Lima, in an attempt to formulate a question frame that was considered socially appropriate and similar to those in common usage, I arrived at the following quote as suitable for informal interviews regarding kin: *¿En que manera estás pariente con el (o ella)?"* ("How are you related to him or her?"). This question is commonly asked by the residents themselves of one another. The reply is consistently in the form of: "She is my mother's sister's daughter," with no mention of relatedness because of a shared grandparent, for example. Thus, in this example, ego thinks of relatedness to another individual in terms of a series of linking relationships that extend out from herself. The relatedness could just as easily have been stated as, "I am related to her because we are both the granddaughters of *X*," a conception which more likely would have been the case in a kin system in which lineality is emphasized. Within the squatter settlements, ego is working within a kindred. He views himself as a central node in a network of kin linked through both males and females.

Depth

Complementary to the ego-centered nature of the kindred in the squatter settlements is the lack of concern with founding ancestors or what Goodenough (1970:43) has called an "ancestor-focus." In the south-central highland village of Chuschi, Isbell (1972:24) found that lineal recognition of ascending generations varied from three to five generations with men recalling further back than women. None of the groups she investigated recognizes a "focal ancestor," nor are there named patrilineages. I suspect that the lack of ancestor focus is fundamental to the nature of an Andean system and not the result of migration or urbanization.

Genealogical information supplied by the residents of Ciudadela Chalaca and Dulanto consistently contains very little genealogical depth. There is very rare mention of descent and much less of ancestors; rather, each individual is concerned with the range of living kin with whom he is allied. Very rarely could an adult recall the names or site of origin beyond the grandparent generation. A few could recall to the fifth generation. Quite often the grandmother's complete name could not be recalled, especially in families in which there had been separation and remarriage. The slight edge in recalling male grandparents and great-grandparents in the squatter settlement is one of the expressions of the patrilateral emphasis. Individuals living in Ciudadela Chalaca and Dulanto, when not able to remember grandparents' or great-grandparents' names, would comment in typically pragmatic fashion to the effect that, "Well, it doesn't really matter since they don't live here in the city," or, "It's not important since they died long ago." Both statements indicate a lack of emphasis placed on those kin who no longer are active participants in ongoing relationships and the stress placed on the extensive kin ties that are presently activated.

In contrast with the generalized lack of depth, the number of kin mentioned in ego's generation and those at least one up and at least one down is extensive, and the linkages are remembered in precise detail. For example, Juan, twenty-one years of age and unmarried, was brought to Ciudadela Chalaca at the age of two. His knowledge of his kin is extensive, though not in any way outstanding or unusual for a man of his age. His knowledge was about equally divided among kin related through his mother's side and through his father's side. He knew no personal names for the great-grandparent generation, though last names could be inferred. At the grandparent generation he knew the full names and some biographical information regarding 10 individuals; for 4 individuals the information was incomplete. At the level of his parents he named and included information on site of birth and present location of 39 individuals. In his own generation, he named and knew detailed personal information regarding 74 kin and supplied additional information on their spouses. At the level below his, he named 34 individuals, all of them living in squatter settlements of the Lima area and most of them very young children or infants. Undoubtedly his naming of the generation younger than his will expand as more children are born to those of his generation. The example provided by the genealogical recall of Juan is typical of the migrants living in Ciudadela Chalaca and Dulanto: there is very little genealogical depth, but extensive emphasis is given to one's own generation and those generations immediately above and below ego.

Those informants who prefaced their discussion of kin with the comment, "I am very poor; I have very few kin," could at least name 150 individuals, while more commonly a typical recall of kin included from 200 to 300, with an emphasis on those residing in the urban areas. At important rites of passage such as weddings or baptisms only rarely were there fewer than 300 people in attendance.

Lack of Respect for the Aged

Another indicator of an emphasis toward bilaterality and the importance of the kindred is the lack of prestige given to the aged for their age *per se* and the tendency to stress association with individuals of the ideally most prosperous, middle-aged years. Among the migrants there is no active recall and respect accorded remote ancestors either as individuals or in a generalized sense. This lack of concern with the remote past and the individuals who were a part of that past is an additional indicator of the very practical concern for the immediate present and aspirations for the future. The emphasis is on the use of present resources in order to arrange for change in the future and not on preservation of a past way of life.

No great prestige is accorded the aged in the squatter settlements. As mentioned previously, very few individuals of advanced age reside in Ciudadela Chalaca or Dulanto. In a sample of 130 families only six individuals were over 60 years of age; most of these were elderly women. Most parents of adults continue to reside in the highlands, a situation which makes day-to-day continuation of obligations impossible. Those middle-aged adults living in the squatter settlement often indicated that one of the considerations which contributed to their decision to migrate from the highlands to the city was to remove themselves from the burden of entangled parental obligations.

The elderly living in the squatter settlement have very little prestige and most often are in a disadvantaged position regarding their control of resources. While most elderly attempt to retain a degree of respect through their continuation of at least a modest level of work and productivity, all those living in Ciudadela Chalaca and Dulanto are dependent on the good will, occasionally only grudgingly given, of their children for their survival. Of those few elderly who had a small individual lot and dwelling before the remodeling, none was included for consideration to receive a lot during the lottery at the time of the remodeling. The loss of homes and lots by the elderly during the remodeling was based on a general consensus among the squatter settlement residents that priority in assigning lots be given to "young, established families" or to "a family with a future." Not only was the community sentiment against the awarding of lots to the elderly, but the elderly did not command enough respect and prestige to reverse, in individual cases, the institutionalized trend to exclude them from obtaining lots. Thus within Ciudadela Chalaca and Dulanto the aged, while often liked for certain personal qualities, are given only a small amount of respect because they are only marginally productive and have very little control of resources.

Additionally, the elderly may retain highland habits such as chewing coca or have dress and linguistic patterns that may be seen as socially undesirable or even embarrassing to some change-oriented sons and daughters. During a social gathering such as a birthday party or the celebration of a saint's fiesta an elderly relative may be given a comfortable chair of respect in order to observe the festivities. Just as likely he may be secluded in the kitchen area or a bedroom and his absence will not be worthy of comment. The elderly are not given special consideration during a conversation, and no particular deference is given to the elderly person who shuffles across a busy street or has trouble walking on uneven ground.

Old age certainly is not viewed as a time of high social prestige or power when compared to middle age. Within the squatter settlements there is no equivalent of "wise elders," nor does there exist any sort of politico-religious group of elders which covertly exerts pressure in community political affairs. In Ciudadela Chalaca between 1965 and 1975 the community members elected to the community council were all middle-aged men.

Descent, Naming, and Inheritance

Descent, naming, and inheritance also contribute some insight into the bilateral nature of kinship in the squatter settlements. Each individual views himself both biologically and socially as descended from both matrilateral and patrilateral kin. Primary value is given to filiation with currently living kin, and this filiation is ideally considered equal for both the male and female side. In many families, because of specific patterns of residence or family business, one side or the other may be emphasized in day-to-day interaction. The tendency to patrilateral emphasis in certain realms will be discussed later.

The procedure for naming and the use of family names is another indicator of the balance that is found between the male and the female kin. The naming system found in the coastal squatter settlements of Peru is similar in general outline to that used throughout Latin America. However, some of its aspects are indicative of general trends and the bilateral emphasis.

Each individual has two sets of names: the personal name (*nombre*) and the family names (*apellidos*). Soon after the birth of a child, a personal name is chosen by either the mother and father jointly or a designated close relative, usually a sibling or an uncle or aunt of the parents of the child. Most parents whose children are born in the squatter settlements search for a name that will be unique, often with urban or modern connotations, and one that has not been recently used by their kin or neighbors. For the migrant women who were born in the highlands common names are Solamina, Apolinaria, Florinda, Domatilda, Obaldina, Illucha, and Claudina, while the men born in the highlands often have names such as Agrapino, Eusabio, Demetrio, Asunción, or Pascual. Younger women and those born in the squatter settlements more often have names which are identified with urban Peru, such as Eva, Carmen, Rosa, Angela, or Julia. The younger men are given names such as Roberto, Hugo, Alfonso, or Carlos. An important influence in the choice of names is the popular media, particularly the daytime soap operas of television and the movies. Thus names such as the following are found in Ciudadela Chalaca and Dulanto — for the girls: Gladys, Elizabeth, Susie, Haydee, and Irma; and for the boys: Maxie, Fidel, Che, Walter, and Popeye. People indicate that ultimately they choose names for their children that they like, that sound good, and that "fit." There are no strong religious or familial strictures for choosing the first name. Most often the choice of names is a creative activity of the parents or close kin. Some individuals also have nicknames, often in reference to a physical characteristic or habit, but the use of nicknames is the exception rather than the rule. Nicknaming is considerably more common among the criollo population than among the highlanders. Some of the nicknames in Ciudadela Chalaca and Dulanto are: *El Loro* (the parrot), *El Gordo* (Fats), *La Niña* (the first female child), and *La Chupitera* (the woman who sells candy). Very commonly a mother will also refer to an infant as *"el bebé"* instead of by name; little children are often addressed as *"mamita"* or *"papito,"* Quechua/Spanish terms of endearment which are the diminutive of the terms for "mother" and "father."

Designation of last names is much more structured than that of personal names. The family name is referred to as the *apellido de mi papá* (father's family name) or *apellido de mi mamá* (mother's family name). Each individual carries the apellido of both the father and the mother. Thus a man's entire name is Efraín (personal name) Flores (father's father's name) Jenebrosa (mother's father's name). And a woman's entire name is Obaldina (personal name) Martínez (father's family name) Sánchez (mother's family name). However, for all practical purposes and in everyday circumstances the personal and father's family name are those commonly used. For example, only for official purposes or when his full name is requested would Efraín mention the name of Jenebrosa. He is known within the squatter settlement and among other highlanders as Efraín Flores. The same pattern is true for women. The residents of Ciudadela Chalaca and Dulanto are aware that for official purposes and government documentation, a woman when she marries is to drop her second apellido (that of her mother) and put in its place that of her husband's father's family preceded by *"de."* Thus on official records when Obaldina and Efraín become man and wife, Obaldina is registered as Obaldina Martínez de Flores. However, in Ciudadela Chalaca and Dulanto among the highlanders the use of the husband's family name after marriage very rarely occurs, and a woman continues to be known by her premarital name: Obaldina Martínez. Because of the strong incest prohibition directed toward marriage between two individuals who share the same apellido, the idea of a man and wife having the same apellido is both amusing and scandalously incongruous. One resident of Ciudadela Chalaca laughed uproariously and commented, "When people are together as a couple and use the same last name, it sounds as though they are brother and sister." Additionally, women in the squatter settlements feel that when they marry or begin to live with men, they do not cease to be who they are, as symbolically represented by a name change, nor do they become part of their husbands' families. Obaldina Martínez will remain Obaldina Martínez until the day she dies, in spite of all the changes and alliances with different men that may have occurred in her lifetime. Women comment that another reason not to change their apellidos is that with marriage they do not cease to be members of their families of orientation, nor may they deny the obligations and the rights which are theirs as members of their families of orientation and particularly of their sibling groups. The few women who on occasion may refer to themselves in the form of "Obaldina de Flores" are viewed as taking on an inappropriate, middle-class affectation.

It is the male apellidos through fathers and sons that are continued through time. The apellido received from the maternal side, which was originally the apellido of one's mother's father and not her mother, is used by a son only during his lifetime and by a daughter only, technically, until she marries. The following diagram (Fig. 5.1) illustrates the principle by which the apellidos Flores and Martínez are carried differently, depending on male or female links. Thus an apellido continues in existence across the generations when it is a male apellido passed from father to son. This dominance of male apellidos is one characteristic of the patrilineal emphasis that is found in the Andes. However, in viewing what actually occurs in the squatter settlements regarding the importance given to apellidos and the functions that they perform, the effects of the patrilateral emphasis are minimal in daily interaction.

Inheritance within the squatter settlements in the late 1970s had not yet become of great concern since the great majority of family heads who came to the city as young couples were still living. There is also not the complicating factor of land ownership, which often is the focus of heated and prolonged litigation in the highlands among survivors after the death of an elderly relative. When premature deaths of adults have occurred in Ciudadela Chalaca and Dulanto, the remaining spouse and children continue to live in the house. Special and beloved goods, or goods obtained before marriage, are distributed by the spouse among the deceased's family of orientation. For example, Eusabio, who died in an automobile accident in 1974, had been a knife sharpener. His wife retained their house, the few furnishings and household utensils, and Eusabio's personal effects. However, his foot-powered whetstone wheel was claimed and obtained by his uncle, a man in his mid-forties and also a knife sharpener by trade. Nevertheless, in some cases severe disagreements have erupted between the spouse of the deceased (particularly if they were *convivientes,* that is, informally living together) and the siblings of the deceased regarding disposition of resources. The successful side is usually the one with the most power in terms of support by extensive kin, paisanos, and extra-kin alliances. In the future, as the age of the heads of households advances, more definite procedures for inheritance are likely to emerge.

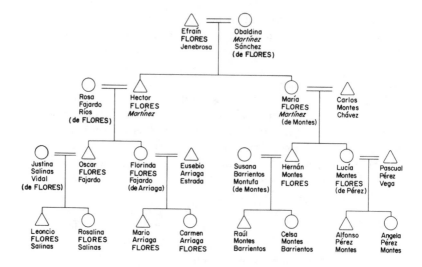

Figure 5.1 Naming principles. The father's family name **(Flores)** continues to be passed from father to son, while the mother's family name *(Martínez)* is passed to only one generation.

Kin as a Network

In a kindred system there is an ego-centered focus, and each kindred is unique so that only siblings potentially (with the exception of one another) share the same kindred. In contrast, "corporateness," such as that found in unilineal descent systems and as discussed by Fox (1967:163), includes "groups that exist independently of the individuals composing them. They exist 'in perpetuity'; individual members come and go, but the group goes on. Corporateness also implies that they act 'as a body'." The descent system which is found in the squatter settlements does not rely on a sense of corporateness but rather on characteristics indicating an ego-centered network of kin.

Each individual living in Ciudadela Chalaca and Dulanto speaks of his kin in terms of "these are my kin." Fernandina says in reference to another person who is pointed out to her, "No, I don't know her; she is not one of us." While standing on the roof of his house, with a view of the surrounding cluster of houses, Hernán, with a sweep of his arm, concludes, "All of these are my relatives; we are all here together." These statements might be construed to indicate the existence of a corporate kin group. However, in exploring each of them one finds that indeed these are typical statements in a society in which each individual is embedded in his individual kin network based on the principles of a kindred. When a person says, "These are my kin," reference is being made to a grouping of kin and not a kin group *per se*. In the squatter settlements the residential clustering of paisanos approaches corporateness vis-à-vis the entire squatter settlement, yet each paisano cluster is made up of numerous overlapping kindreds in which there is some contiguous residency among siblings. Paisanos are the most inclusive group with which each individual is associated. All one's paisanos may be considered as "us" as opposed to non-paisanos who are viewed as "them." To each individual the paisano grouping is an identity group which not incidentally includes, but is not limited to, all of that individual's kin. Thus there is a residential group and an identity group which is composed of overlapping individual kindreds but which does not function in its entirety as a corporate group. The fundamental kin grouping is in the form of the ego-centered kindred. The residence pattern and the existence of the paisano groupings are factors which provide a deceptively corporate expression, though not function, to interaction.

SIBLING SOLIDARITY

The fact of shared kindreds among siblings is a critical component in sibling solidarity. Only a set of siblings is able to function as a group of individuals through a shared kindred. Additionally, only a set of siblings is able to work together to fulfill an obligation or to obtain the same rights vis-à-vis a common relative to whom they are related through the same linkages. Only siblings are able to view the panorama of their kindred as the same and yet unique from that of all other nonsiblings. Their shared kindreds carry implications of similar sets of relationships. For example, in a bilateral kindred system, not only would an uncle and his nephew have some quite different members within each of their kindreds, but even more of a contrast would be their distinctive statuses in relation to shared kin. However, in contrast, a set of siblings shares not only the members of each other's kindreds, but to a very large extent all hold the same status relationship with these shared kin. The primary distinction among siblings is birth order. Thus, in the ideal model of an ego-centered, bilateral kindred, there is a structural basis for a set of siblings to share certain concerns, viewpoints, and potential relationships. Within the Peruvian squatter settlements this structural basis underlies much of the observed behavior of sets of siblings.

In addition to the structural principles that encourage sibling solidarity, there are also a number of other cultural factors related to the process of urbanization that contribute to defining and maintaining the basic sibling unit. In the squatter settlement the sibling unit is the basis for identity and adaptation, and for stability, well-being, and prestige-building. Sentiments regarding the importance of the sibling tie are often expressed both as statements of an ideal and as behavioral patterns.

An indicator as to the ideal strength of the sibling bond is found in the response to a commonly asked question: *"¿Cuántos son ustedes?"* ("How many of you are there [in this household or family]?"), which is often inquired by adults of children with whom they are initiating a conversation. The almost predictable response is, for example, *"Somos cinco"* ("We are five"), indicating that there are "five of us" — not including the parents but only the five siblings. Likewise an adult, while seated in his home in the presence of his spouse and children, would almost unhesitatingly respond to the same question to the effect that he and his siblings are so many in number, perhaps adding that here in the house there are four children and his spouse.

Alfonso, who is in his mid-thirties and has lived in Lima almost fifteen years, is one of a five-member sibling group which along with spouses and families settled originally in Ciudadela Chalaca. Regarding his siblings, Alfonso commented, "It is important for brothers and sisters to stick together, mainly so that there will be mutual aid. For this one needs harmony. For example, if I am visiting my brother and am offered some food, I must accept it so as to not reject this kind gesture on his part. If there is any problem, Elio [the oldest brother] comes over to get us and we leave 'to fight the war.' " His wife Florinda, the oldest of seven siblings, who had worked when a teenager as a live-in maid for a wealthy family, added,

> I think that the idea of people helping one another because they are siblings is something that poor people living in the squatter settlement do. Among the rich people, they all have their own lives. However, our family [referring to herself and her siblings] is different. Although there may be disagreements, Isabel, José, and I are just alike and we will do anything to help one another. Even with the others [four half-siblings, each with a different father], we all consider one another siblings and help one another.

An individual who cannot count on many kin, especially siblings or first cousins, to come to his aid in time of need is indeed disadvantaged. Again and again the residents of the squatter settlements commented to this effect, stressing that "we could not survive here in the city were it not for the aid of our siblings at those times when we really need it." By the mid-1960s it was very rare, almost unheard of, for a migrant or a migrant family to settle in a squatter settlement without at least one sibling or near cousin also present.

In the extremely rare instance in which an individual finds himself in the city with no siblings at hand, there are two strategies that can be employed. If first cousins or other close cousins live in the city, they may be treated as siblings and their role extended to include many of the rights and duties ordinarily found to exist among siblings. The second arrangement is to marry into a family in which there are numerous and cooperative siblings who exhibit a strong sense of unity. Such a strategy is advantageous to the in-marrying person, who may come from a position of relative powerlessness in the absence of a sibling group. This arrangement is also often preferred by the strong sibling group, as it assures a high degree of allegiance on the part of the in-marrying affine.

It is the ideal pattern for groups of siblings and their families of procreation to migrate within a period of a few years of one another, settle near one another, aid one another in the initial period of settling in, and help find employment for one another. This core relationship, along with the nuclear family of procreation, forms the basis of support and aid during the process of urbanization. Many of the cooperative efforts among siblings that are found in the rural Peruvian highlands have been modified to fulfill urban survival needs. This continuity — at times an intensification of forms of relationship that existed in the highlands — is one of the factors that mitigates against the "isolation" and "disorganization" so often associated with the process of urbanization.

Arrival in the City

The most common place for a new migrant to stay upon his arrival in the city is with a sibling or other close relative. This initial period of settling in may last from a few days to weeks, months, or even years. By the late 1960s, with more than one-third of the population of Lima in squatter settlements, it was the very rare new migrant indeed who did not have at least one sibling living in a squatter settlement. If not a sibling, then certainly a first cousin, uncle, or aunt would provide temporary shelter. This pattern of moving in with close kin already living in a squatter settlement when the migrant arrives in the city is in contrast to reports by Matos (1966b:83) and

Alers and Applebaum (1968:8) to the effect that most migrants first live in inner-city slums and only later move to squatter settlements. Mangin (1973:318) has observed that "more people are coming directly to the *barriadas* from the provinces, often upon the advice and with the assistance of relatives and others from the same region."

Some of the first relatively small groups of initiators of new squatter settlements through invasion may have lived some time in inner-city tenements, but the large number of yearly immigrants from the highlands to the coast could not nearly begin to find space in the relatively small tenement district of downtown Lima. The strong patterns of kin and particularly sibling obligation and hospitality would make it highly unlikely for a newly arrived migrant to settle anywhere except with or near already-settled siblings or other kin. Many families who have moved to Dulanto since 1973 and who are now in the process of constructing their homes admit that when their houses are completed it will become much more difficult to make temporary additions for visiting kin than was the case in Ciudadela Chalaca.

As Justina said in reference to two of her husband's teenage first cousins who had stayed with them for the past seven months, "No, of course we could not charge them anything. But we know their family will always do the same for us when we visit the highlands." The expectation of providing shelter for newly arriving or visiting kin, especially siblings, is an obligation which one expects reciprocated as soon as the proper occasion arises.

While living with established siblings, the newly arrived migrants receive a great deal of often subtle yet vital transitional advice and support. This is the time when changes in clothing will be initiated. Perhaps a woman will decide to cut her braids, a symbol of the Andean highlands, in favor of a short urban hairstyle. During the settling-in period the migrants become accustomed to a world in which Spanish is spoken in almost all situations. The recent migrants also learn from their host families the primary bus routes which will be of use to them and the location in the city of vital shops, marketplaces, and government agencies or facilities. The newly arrived young children are taken by their experienced cousins to the local school and are brought into the circle of kin and paisano playmates who, if the family ultimately settles in this squatter settlement, will accompany them throughout their youth.

Often young unmarried siblings in their teens make visits from the highlands that may extend for months in order to "try the city out," to attend school, or to earn some money for a specific purchase that is

needed in the highlands. These long-term visitors, who have no immediate plans of establishing themselves in the city on a permanent
basis, most commonly also stay with already-established siblings living
in the squatter settlements. Young men who have been drafted into
the armed forces from the highlands often stay at the home of a sibling
in a squatter settlement during free periods. A parallel situation is
found among young women who work as live-in servants in the more
elegant districts of Lima and stay with siblings or other close kin
during their days off.

The strength of community consensus that siblings and other
near kin are obligated to care for newly arrived highland migrants is
illustrated in the case of Virginia and Lorenzo, who in 1969 had lived
in Ciudadela Chalaca for six years. There arrived in Ciudadela Chalaca
a young migrant family. The wife, who spoke only very little Spanish,
was due to give birth within the next few weeks. No member of this
family had ever been in the city before and consequently they were
in a very dependent situation. Among their kin, Virginia (who was a
half-sister to the husband) and Lorenzo had decided to take them in until they could find a place of their own. Their day of arrival in Ciudadela
Chalaca was a time of some excitement among their kinsmen, and
Lorenzo and his oldest son went to the bus terminal to meet them and
accompany them in a taxi to Ciudadela Chalaca. The newly arrived
family brought numerous sacks of belongings and gifts of food. When
they arrived in Ciudadela Chalaca and stepped from the taxi, their
appearance — the husband in a dark suit and the wife in well-braided
hair, a long red skirt, and bright pink sweater — was a contrast to
Lorenzo and his son, who were dressed in sport shirts, sweaters, and
stylish slacks. Virginia, with her short waved hair, sweater, and loose
cotton skirt, met them at the door of their home and presented a contrast to her country sister-in-law. On descending from the taxi and
unloading their belongings from the top, the newly arrived family
stood for a moment dazed by their surroundings. However, they were
rapidly and warmly welcomed into the home of Lorenzo and Virginia
and in the afternoon made visits to other kin and paisanos who lived
nearby. After two weeks the children had begun school and the family
had learned the basics of urban survival. However, the husband, a car-
penter, had not yet found employment, nor had his wife given birth.
One night during a loud argument Virginia, who is known for her
strong and opinionated character, expelled the newcomers, saying
that they had stayed too long, that it was costing her family too much
to feed them, that the husband would never find a job, and that
besides they had never really been close as a brother and sister. The

newly arrived family moved in with other relatives, the wife's first cousins, who lived three doors away. When news of these events reached their mutual kin within Ciudadela Chalaca, it was met with shock and negative sanction of Virginia's actions. The expulsion of a family of visiting kin, particularly one with so few urban skills and expecting the birth of a child soon, was scandalous. In the following months Virginia was made to pay by being shunned at the community water spigot used by most of her kin and paisanos as well as by partial exclusion from some kin activities and celebrations. Meanwhile, true to her reputation, Virginia defended her action to the end. The newly arrived family after some months obtained a source of income and built their own house on a small vacant piece of land. Five years later in 1974 this event was still referred to as a disgraceful occurrence among kin.

Residence Pattern

In a squatter settlement such as Ciudadela Chalaca in which population growth is characterized by gradual accretion over the years rather than by invasion, there was by the late 1960s a generalized and quite evident tendency for siblings and other close kinsmen to be residentially clustered. For example, residents of Ciudadela Chalaca often commented that in looking for paisanos or former residents of their home villages in an unfamiliar squatter settlement, the most efficient procedure is to enter the settlement and ask the first friendly-looking passerby where, for instance, people from the province of Ancash live. Once in the vicinity in which those from Ancash are found, one should ask for the area in which those from the district of, say, Huari live; once the more specific residential area has been located, then one should enquire where those from the specific village live. Thus, in most squatter settlements there is a tendency for residential patterning to be a reconstituted microcosm of the geographic-political divisions found in the highlands.

Ciudadela Chalaca, from the time of its inception until its remodeling in 1973, was characterized by a steady increase in house structures and population density. During this period a settlement pattern was established in which siblings' houses were often contiguous or near one another within a paisano cluster. After the remodeling, in which lots were regularized in size and possession, the establishment of new houses by migrant families was slowed considerably, continuing only on a very small, undercover basis. At the time of the remodeling a number of these original, sibling, residential blocks were dispersed.

Much of the informal daily interchange within the squatter
settlements among sibling groupings is between women.

The drawing of lots was organized so that residents of one sector
most often remained within the same but reordered sector after the
remodeling. The sibling groupings in 1974 did not re-form the residentially cohesive groupings which had existed previous to the remodeling, when Ciudadela Chalaca was settled in the pattern most congenial to the migrants' needs.

Daily Informal Interchange

Because of the close residential proximity of siblings and other
near kin, patterns of trust, and the long-established reciprocal obligations, a good deal of daily interaction occurs between nuclear families
linked by sibling ties. Relationships among families linked by sibling

ties are defined by exchange based on reciprocity rather than by the sharing of goods and services, as might be more common in a unilineal corporate group. A great deal of mutual support exists, particularly as each sibling understands that his or her sibling will likewise lend support, either moral or material, in times of need. Since many of the men work outside the squatter settlement during the day, while the women who have small children tend to work either in the local market or are self-employed within the squatter settlement, much of the informal daily interchange among siblings is between women: between siblings themselves, *cuñadas* (siblings-in-law), such as between ego and her spouse's female sibling or between ego's and her male sibling's spouse; or between *con-cuñadas* (between ego and her spouse's male sibling's spouse). These interchanges include primarily the short-term borrowing of cooking and household utensils and of clothing, the exchange of child-care tasks, and occasionally, especially during times of crisis, the exchange of tasks such as washing clothes or preparing food. The daily informal interchange among men who are siblings, first cousins, cuñados, or con-cuñados consists of reciprocal aid in house construction and repair; reciprocal "treating" and toasting of one another in the purchase of beer; the loaning of tools, a bicycle, or cash; or collaboration in a business enterprise.

Special Occasions

The sibling tie is also particularly evident during rites of intensification, rites of passage, and other periods of social crisis or importance. For example, Lola comments that at the birthday party of adults it is the "obligation" for all siblings to attend. Additionally, it is siblings and affines linked through siblings who provide most of the emotional support as well as material aid during such life-crisis situations as childbirth and death. The sibling units also often play a vital role in the sponsoring of fiestas and in the makeup of soccer and volleyball teams.

FAMILY RELATIONSHIPS

CHAPTER 6

One day in 1974 in Ciudadela Chalaca a long-time resident whom I had known since 1964 pointed to a genealogical diagram that I was completing and observed that, although he well understood the method I was using, a diagram would make much more sense if conceptualized in the manner that he could easily show me. He then proceeded to diagram a kinship scheme which was in the next months repeated consistently and almost precisely by numerous other residents of Ciudadela Chalaca and Dulanto. This scheme is a diagrammatic representation of the squatter settlement residents' conceptualization of their kinship system characterized by ranks of concentric circles radiating out from a centrally located ego (Fig. 6.1). The scheme of concentric circles is not a unique one. In reference to the Andean highlands, for example, Custred (1977) uses a model of concentric circles which shares numerous features with the model discussed here. A model of kinship that is based on a series of concentric circles radiating out from a centralized ego is generally associated with societies in which bilaterality and the kindred are basic concepts, as is the case in the squatter settlements of Lima.

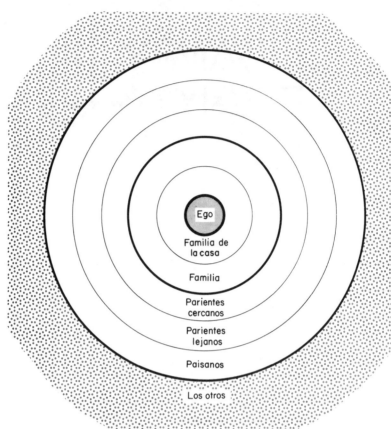

Figure 6.1 Model of social structure, as designed and
corroborated by squatter settlement residents, show-
ing ego at the center of a kindred.

At this point it is necessary to clarify the schematic shorthand
represented by the model. The model is the same for both men and
women. Some variation occurs between those who are married and
those who are unmarried. At the center of the model is ego, unique
and alone and ultimately separated from all other individuals. In the
first circle, closest to ego, is the category given the label *familia de la
casa* (family of the house). To most informants the familia de la casa
includes spouse and children if ego is married, and parents and siblings
if ego is not married. If ego is married the familia de la casa may also
include, to some, siblings; although siblings, especially married siblings, usually do not live in the same house with ego, they nevertheless

constitute the core of kin closest to ego in various regards. Those who did not include siblings in the familia de la casa included them in the next level, *familia* (family). This variation as to the placement of siblings among married informants is a reflection of the often only partially resolved ambivalence of the sibling tie when juxtaposed with the marriage tie. The next level or rank distant from ego is that category of kin labeled *familia,* which includes (if ego is married) ego's married siblings, parents, grandparents, and parents' and grandparents' siblings (and perhaps their children). For all informants it includes both patrilateral and matrilateral second cousins; some included third cousins. Familia also includes siblings' children as well as the children of first and second cousins (and sometimes third cousins) and grandchildren if these no longer live in the same house as ego. Familia de la casa and familia are often lumped and referred to as *mi familia* (my family), as these are the kin with whom ego interacts most frequently and with whom the most effective bonds are felt. The circles of kin beyond familia are divided from familia by a rather more distant boundary than that between the other concentric circles.

In the next circle are found the *parientes cercanos* (near kin). The term *parientes* also has a more generalized meaning in reference to kin in general. Thus, one may ask someone, *"¿Es pariente con ella?"* in the sense of, "Are you related to her?" so that all kin may be referred to as *parientes,* yet not all parientes are familia. Parientes cercanos include the cousins beyond second or third cousins, the kin termed *tíos* (that is, uncles and aunts), yet whose exact linkage is somewhat vague or more distant than parents' siblings. The implication is that in a time of crisis or in the absence of members of one's familia the parientes cercanos may often be called to the fore.

Beyond the parientes cercanos are the *parientes lejanos* (distant kin), whose exact link of kin affiliation may be fuzzy to each individual ego but who are considered parientes nevertheless, either because of a shared apellido or because they were mentioned at some time by a close relative as also being related, though often through an unclear link. Thus parientes lejanos must be considered as kin, yet they interact with ego most commonly in the more formalized gatherings of "all the kin," such as at a wake or a wedding.

Beyond the real kin lies a diffuse area of those individuals termed *paisanos,* that is, those originating from the same highland district as ego. However, many persons are quick to point out that there is a common belief that being paisanos is almost like being kin. It is also generally believed that in many cases if descent were traced far enough and with enough care that "in the end we would all be related in one way or another with all of our paisanos." *Paisano* and *pariente* are inclusive terms in that all parientes and familia are likewise paisanos to ego yet not all paisanos are parientes or familia. Preference is given to use of the terms *parientes* and *familia* if these ties indicating closeness are present. It is the paisano grouping that is often referred to as *nosotros* (us) within the squatter settlements; those who are not paisanos are *ellos* (them) or *los otros* (the others). Clearly, beyond *paisano* is the line separating the kin, the geographically specific identity group, from those who are considered alien and potentially threatening.

Within this scheme, affines present a special consideration. Strictly speaking, to most residents of the squatter settlements, affines are not kin and most certainly are not considered a part of the individual's kindred. Nevertheless, affines are viewed as related to one through a marriage link. Some of those residents of Ciudadela Chalaca and Dulanto who discussed this model added the affines after the consanguineal kin had been clearly established. Thus, spouses of ego are placed in the familia de la casa, and spouses of siblings and all of those found in the rank familia are placed in the familia. Likewise, spouses of those found in the parientes cercanos and parientes lejanos levels might also be included there by some informants. However, all informants were careful to point out that affines are not one's kin but rather cuñados or con-cuñados and would be included on a diagram of relatives primarily because they are the spouses of kin and the parents of kinsmen.

FAMILIA DE LA CASA

In the squatter settlements the unit defined with the label *familia de la casa* is both the domestic unit and in most cases the nuclear family. The nuclear family of procreation is the basic kin, domestic, and economic unit in the squatter settlements. It is most often the young nuclear family, consisting of the husband, the wife, and the young children, that migrates to the city. After a variable period of time in which this family unit usually resides with kin until settled, it is the nuclear family which, if at all possible, will eventually establish its own home.

Although construction materials and close proximity inhibit total privacy and separateness, there is a strong sense of the need to fulfill certain daily functions within one's own home. It is within individual households, in which resides the nuclear family of procreation, that daily preparation and consumption of food is carried out, and that sleeping, procreation, dressing, and storage of personal effects all occur. There is a strong feeling that, ideally, all of these domestic functions should be carried out in a separate household in which reside the spouses and their children. However, as indicated earlier, because of long-term visiting kin and the difficulty of finding space for new houses for newly married couples, this ideal is very often not a reality. It is the rare household which does not include at least one person who is not a member of the family of procreation. For example, when the conversation comes to the question of how many live in her house, Justina quite typically says, "Just my husband and I and our three children live here. This is our house. However, my sister, her husband, and two children have been staying with us for the last three months until they find a lot." The anthropologist asks, "And the young man whom I see here sometimes in the evenings?" Justina replies, "That's my husband's nephew who is in the army. He just comes here to sleep on the weekends when he has time off." Thus, although the actual number of persons sleeping and eating in a household may fluctuate over a period of time, the migrants view a basic household unit as consisting of the spouses and their children.

Economic Arrangements

The nuclear family of procreation within the setting of the squatter settlement is also the basic economic unit of production and consumption. Often both the male and female heads of a household, as well as some of the older children, work and earn money. Between the husband and wife, particularly, there is common talk of "my business," "my job," or "my profession." Women who more often than men are involved in commercial enterprises which entail initial investments and management of stock, are careful to point out that "this is money that I earn." There is a great deal of variation in the degree to which the income of both of the spouses is pooled to form a general family income. It is the rare adult who does not earn at least some income, however modest it may be. Thus every household generally has a number of sources of income. In some families the husband, who may be the primary wage-earner, keeps the exact sum of his earnings a secret and gives his wife what is called a *diario* (daily allowance) that he estimates necessary to cover household expense. This type of arrangement is often openly and vociferously criticized by women in the squatter settlements whenever they become aware of its existence within a particular family. The criticism is leveled at the man who would first not reveal to his wife the exact sum of his earnings and then not share with his wife the decision-making venture of allocating family expenses. Finally, a husband who does not share economic decisions with his spouse is often stereotypically suspected by the women in the community of keeping an inordinate proportion of his wages for himself which he is then suspected or accused of spending for beer on the weekends, to the deprivation of the wife and children and the ultimate detriment of the family unit. It is primarily the most urban and criollo families in which this type of division of economic arrangement occurs, and only among the coastal criollo families do men express the opinion that women should not work but must stay in the home and care for the children, a pattern conforming closely to the urban middle-class ideal.

In most families in which the female members are not secluded and in which a positive desire is expressed for hard work for all, there is a fairly egalitarian view of the sharing of economic responsibilities and of earnings. In these families both men and women work and share with one another a knowledge of their earnings. They also pool their earnings for joint goals of the family unit. Visiting kin who reside within the house are excluded from the family pooling of resources. They have to pay for their own food and other expenses although they are given a free place to live.

In another type of economic arrangement there is a great deal of independence among family members regarding their individual incomes and jobs. In this case the woman is responsible for her own clothing and the expenses of the children, as well as for most of the food expenses for the entire family. The husband is responsible for his own personal expenses and some of the family expenses such as shoes for the children, while both the husband and wife save either jointly or individually for large expenses such as house construction or large appliances. When there are strong ties and equally strong obligations toward a sibling group, there is a tendency or at least a leaning toward an independence of income so that expensive obligations toward one's siblings may be met with money which has been earned by oneself and which is thought of as one's own. This type of economic arrangement within the family is a reflection of the general balancing and ambivalence regarding one's obligations to the family of procreation and to one's siblings.

The degree to which incomes should be shared and pooled for joint goals is an area of contention in some nuclear families. As a final bomb-blast in a family argument in Ciudadela Chalaca a woman shouted at her husband whom she felt was not sharing the economic load, "You only come here to eat, sleep, fuck, and shit." Likewise the

Selling prepared foods in front of her home,
this vendor adds to the household income.

ultimatum in a family argument came when the wife told her husband
in straightforward terms, "This is my house. I bought the wood and
the tin roof myself with my own earnings. The bed and table are mine,
too. If you don't like what you find here, then go." Thus, while the
relationship between spouses within the nuclear family of procreation
is not entirely an economic arrangement, nor are the above examples
to suggest that strife is a general characteristic of conjugal interaction,
yet a fundamental premise is that a marriage or the act of living
together as *convivientes* obligates both parties into a web of binding
and extensive reciprocal expectations. Many conjugal obligations are
viewed in economic terms. Emotional support is a given between
spouses or comes from the sibling tie. The economic concerns in a
marriage must be bartered, coerced, and continually monitored, tallied,
and reevaluated.

Because each individual is at the center of a network of relationships, the marriage responsibility, albeit an important one, is but one of
multiple social responsibilities, many of them including economic
expectations. For example, while married siblings do not pool their

incomes for day-to-day expenses, it is very common for siblings to work as a group in undertakings which are often extremely expensive, such as the sponsorship of the fiesta of a patron saint, the care of a sick relative, extensive travel for one or all of them, or joint legal suits against another party. These joint activities carried out by a group of siblings are often undertaken with the expectation of eventually building prestige or economic gain for the entire sibling group as well as through a sense of duty to act in unity.

Sexual Complementarity

Within Ciudadela Chalaca and Dulanto there are almost exclusively no single-sex households. Young unmarried youths do not form separate households with other youths; they stay in their family of orientation until they marry and, because of the scarcity of vacant lots in the squatter settlements, they often remain in the parental household after marriage. Middle-aged, unmarried bachelors or spinsters do not live alone but attach themselves to another household. Separated or widowed adults with small children may manage alone for a short time, but as soon as possible they will form another conjugal union or as a last resort will live with parents or other close kin. Single men, particularly those with young children, are in greater need of joining another family because of the prohibition against the preparation of food by men. The setting up of nuclear-family households is the result primarily of the felt need for a "real" home to consist of at least a couple and their children. An individual living alone is nearly inconceivable and would be seen as perversely unnatural, because each person, while an individual, is identified as a member of a grouping of kin, the smallest unit of which is the nuclear family of procreation.

In the familia de la casa some of the fundamental obligations and expectations of responsibility are based on a division of labor by sex and by age and on an adherence to the values of industriousness and responsibility to one's family. Both a man and a woman are seen as necessary and complementary to the smooth functioning of each household. This sexual complementarity is also found in the highland community of Chuschi: "One is necessarily female and the other male. They are complements or 'the essential other halves' of one another; the combination of the two is necessary for life to continue, for time to move and for the Andean world to be understood" (Isbell 1974:13).

In the squatter settlements the position of men and women is expressed as ideally being egalitarian with an emphasis on family prosperity through cooperative effort and hard work. Interestingly, Isbell (1974) concludes her discussion of the pattern of sexual complementarity in the highlands with a noted change to a less egalitarian situation where there is contact with more Western concepts. Migrants with long-term contact with the city and such urban practices as a lower industrial minimum wage for women, though, may feel some pressure to shift toward a less sexually egalitarian relationship between the spouses. In the late 1970s, however, the relationship maintained by the migrants in the squatter settlements, compared to that among the criollo and middle-class urban populations, was strikingly egalitarian. However, within the squatter settlements one finds a continuum of modes of relationship, ranging from very egalitarian households to those which closely approximate the more urban, middle-class norms, including the complex of machismo and the economically dependent and socially secluded woman. In the squatter settlements almost all of the women in migrant families are expected to be, and in fact are, to some degree economically independent. Some are also social organizers and leaders within paisano groupings. Women in the squatter settlements often point out that it is the woman of the family who must be strong both physically and morally because it is she who must bear the children and work for these children in the day-to-day struggle. Men and women must be equally practical and hard-headed in economic matters and in facing the vagaries of life. Each woman as well as each man must be prepared at any time to carry on without a spouse should the occasion arise. These are not only ideal statements, for the daily reality is that most household units consist of men and women, both of whom are diligent and industrious workers and neither of whom is considered socially or economically inferior to the other, in contrast to the Latin American stereotype of male dominance and female seclusion and passivity.

The reactions to the television soap operas illustrate something of sex roles. For example, the personalities of the characters diverge sharply from the experience of the migrants in one important aspect. The women in the novelas, particularly those shows produced in Mexico, are generally depicted as being passive and long-suffering. The migrant women in the squatter settlements very often find these character traits both amusing and disgustingly absurd, commenting that "we Peruvians are not like *that*." During an episode in which a female character was passively accepting verbal abuse from her lover, the six women and their children watching the program coached the actress with advice such as "Give him a good one" and "Get him." After the program one woman commented with disgust, "That was so ridiculous that she would let him treat her like that. No one will respect a woman like that."

Vibrantly strong characters are not the exclusive domain of

either sex. While for men this strength of character is often shown through expressions of power in elaborate displays of wealth at appropriate celebrations or in the mobilization of support through the formation of reciprocal alliances, women more often exhibit their strength of character through verbal expression, intense physical activity, and nonpassive, social interaction. A sustained struggle for what is due one's family is seen as a very positive attribute of both men and women, while passivity in defending one's rights is viewed as a weakness.

In the Peruvian squatter settlements food and its preparation and service are symbolically powerful elements that give some insight into sex roles and the interaction of members of the family of procreation. The topic of the purchase, preparation, and consumption of food is a common one in daily conversation. Nostalgic recollections by the migrants in reference to the highlands revolve around the plentiful amount of food available, the wide variety of potatoes and meats, and the delicious preparation of specialty dishes served during fiestas and other celebrations. For individuals who spent their youth in the highlands heftiness is generally equated with strength. A woman is considered not only physically attractive if she is *bien gordita* (nicely plump) but also — even more importantly — physically strong. Likewise, babies and small children are admired and thought to be strong and healthy if they are gorditos, or plump. A whispered insult behind a mother's back is that her child is "so tiny and thin, a nothing."

Among residents of the squatter settlements, but especially among the women, since food acquisition and preparation is primarily their domain, a topic of daily concern is the shifting price of basic foodstuffs and the concomitant quality of food offered by a particular vendor in the local marketplace. One of the bases for the almost absolute absence of single-sexed households and one of the most pervasive examples of the division of labor by sex is found in the taboo against the preparation of food by men. Food preparation and service is a symbol par excellence of a woman's role and expectations within the familia de la casa. At informal family meals the women of the household serve the food, deciding on the amount for each recipient. When a plate is emptied, the woman who has prepared the food will initiate a second helping by requesting if the recipient would like more. If the recipient declines more food, the woman who is serving may decide that he or she should have more anyway, and she will place more on the plate with a comment such as, "You need more; you have worked hard." The recipient will generally refrain from protest and consume what has been given him or her. In the large meal of the day,

A woman and her eldest daughter prepare the large
midday meal.

served traditionally soon after noon, there are two dishes served con-
secutively, a large soup dish and then a dish of rice, potatoes, or manioc
with beans or meat. Thus the routine of service and potential refill
will be repeated twice in a meal for every member of the family at the
table. The timing and the amount of food served is under the complete
control of the woman who has prepared the meal. The rest of the
family sits passively by as the woman exercises her prerogative as the

provider of sustenance. In a more formal setting, such as a fiesta or a meal for guests, the woman who has prepared the food generally eats in the kitchen often with her other female helpers, either during the meal or shortly thereafter. This strict division between the area of preparation and the area of consumption, between those who give and those who receive, leads to a social and physical boundary between the giver and the receiver.

The woman who prepares and serves food is not seen in a subservient role as one who provides a service to others; on the contrary, since she is in control of the family's food, so symbolically representative of wealth, prestige, and power in a general sense, she is the initiator and controller of wealth in the form of vital sustenance. At mealtimes she demonstrates her power as well as her absolute control of a reciprocal offering in turn for which she expects a variety of resources in the form of time and money from the other family members. Thus the preparation and serving of food by female members of a household is a prime example of the division of labor by sex and the need for cooperation between men and women.

FAMILIA

As mentioned previously, both familia de la casa and the more generalized familia, although they consist of different kin, are lumped for certain situations and may be referred to jointly as *mi familia*. The primary distinguishing criterion between familia de la casa and familia is membership or lack of membership in the same household as ego. The circles of kin beyond familia are divided from familia by a more distinct boundary than that which exists between familia de la casa and familia. It is between these two divisions that the most flexibility in extension of roles and substitution of actors exists.

For a married adult the familia includes parents, grandparents, first and second (or third) cousins, paternal and maternal aunts and uncles, and nieces and nephews. As previously mentioned, siblings may be included here with familia or they may be placed within the rank which is closer to ego. For the unmarried ego, familia includes all of the above kin excluding siblings and parents, who are a part of the familia de la casa. Thus with marriage, one's spouse and subsequent children become a part of the inner rank, while parents and perhaps siblings are placed in a rank further removed from ego.

The level of the familia is the boundary for the incest taboo. A very strong generalized incest prohibition exists within la familia which is explained on the grounds that (1) one may not marry within the same apellido, and (2) one may not marry *primos hermanos* or *primos de segundo grado* (second cousins). These are marriage prohibition rules which were clearly stated by residents of the squatter settlements again and again during discussions of the formation of alliances through marriage. Because every individual carries two apellidos, one from the maternal side and one from the paternal side, any ego will necessarily share with all of those found in his familia at least one apellido, or the apellido carried by a mother or grandmother, thus excluding potential marriage among familia members. Likewise, apellidos may also commonly be shared by ego and an individual outside the familia, thus also tending toward a prohibition of marriage. Yet kin within familia always share apellidos and thus are always excluded from the choice of marriage partners. Kin who are beyond familia and who do not share apellidos may be potential marriage partners, although some social disapproval may be expressed if relatedness is known to be "close."

Grandparents

Grandparents are rarely present within the squatter settlements because of the general absence of elderly persons. Only in the 1970s, with the first few marriages among the children, has a grandparent generation begun to emerge. Grandparents — especially grandmothers, who have much more contact with grandchildren than do grandfathers — treat their grandchildren much in the same commanding way that parents do, insisting that they remain obedient and complete their chores. Grandparents may on occasion spank grandchildren with the same vehemence as the parents. Even as the grandchildren near adulthood, a grandparent, particularly if of very strong and commanding character, may demand good behavior on the part of a grandchild. For example, once at a three-day fiesta for the patron saint of a paisano group, Alejo, a young man who had been drinking a good deal, called rather roughly across the room to his grandmother to share a drink with him. His grandmother, Claudencia, who is in her mid-seventies, came up to him and began to roughly pull his hair saying, "How disrespectful. Be careful: do not act that way." She slapped him lightly on the face and then said, "Give me your money so I can buy my medicines." She then reached into his pocket and took out his money, and he sheepishly went back to the side of the room where the men were sitting. The participants in the fiesta watched the interchange with amusement.

Conversely, grandparents may be affectionate, lenient, and teasing with grandchildren in a way that parents seldom are. Grandparents often give their grandchildren sweets and carry them in their arms long after a mother has ceased to do so. Often, too, it is mentioned that grandparents and grandchildren "make jokes" with one another. For example, the grandmother calls her small grandson her "husband" or asks him if he wants to marry her.

Cousins

In most instances and in daily interaction primos (whether primos hermanos or second or third cousins) belong to the familia by virtue of their only rarely sharing a domestic household with ego. The unity of members of the same generational level is demonstrated by the extensive daily interaction among primos who interact as age-mates and companions. For example, children who are primos often play together and attend school together, often sharing books and supplies if they are in the same classroom. As adults, primos are those who are included in large-scale family celebrations such as baptisms or wakes. Primos are those individuals after siblings to whom ego will turn for aid and support. The implications of the strong sibling tie are numerous at the structural level. Within the squatter settlements the bond between primos hermanos is very strong; in many instances an individual primo hermano may interact with ego almost as a sibling would. If there are not enough siblings in the city for reciprocal house construction, a primo hermano will be asked to help. If siblings cannot accumulate the resources necessary for the sponsorship of a fiesta or a large celebration, the primos hermanos will also be recruited into the effort. Usually soccer teams include siblings, primos hermanos, and perhaps other kin and paisanos.

The ties found between siblings and first cousins and other kin are reflected in some of the kinship terminology. In Quechua the same term is used both for siblings and for children of one's parent's siblings. Although the great majority of those living in the squatter settlements speak Spanish for everyday purposes and many of the younger generation know very little Quechua, the bond between ego and first cousins is similar to the tie reflected in the Quechuan terminology. Often in the squatter settlements primos hermanos refer to one another in a casual context as *hermanos*, that is, brothers or siblings, and only after direct questioning is it revealed that the kin tie is one of parent's sibling's child and not brother. The use of *hermano* is frequently justified by "Ever since we were children, we have been close, just like brothers." In daily interaction this closeness is not surprising, particularly if the parents of both individuals also have a close relationship and perhaps reside near one another.

It is common for siblings and primos to play together
daily as in this group playing house.

Likewise, cross-generationally, a group of adult siblings who
frequently interact as neighbors in the squatter settlements present a
block of *tíos* and *tías* (uncles and aunts) to whom the subsequent generation of children, who are all primos hermanos to one another, may
look for advice, support, and solace in the absence of their parents.
As a lifetime of reciprocal obligation has passed between the set of
siblings who are now parents, a certain degree of obligation exists
for an aunt or uncle to extend some aid to his sibling's children, particularly within the squatter settlement when the true parent may be
in the highlands. Aid is most often in the form of assistance in locating
employment, in being accepted in a specialized educational program, or
in securing a lot in a squatter settlement. The sibling unit is a basic
dyadic core from which many other relationships are extended outward.

Children of ego's parent's sibling's child (children of primo hermano) often are referred to with the same term (*sobrino*) as that used
for ego's sibling's child and are included within the general category
of nieces and nephews. This lumping of kin categories is another
indication of the close bond often found between ego and a primo
hermano.

At the level of second or third cousins, interaction may be somewhat attenuated on a daily basis. Nevertheless, these kin are familia,
and ego recognizes this kin tie and the importance of activating obligations and responsibilities in the proper situations. The relationship
between ego and second and third cousins is similar to that between
ego and primos hermanos, only progressively more distant and diffuse.

Aunts and Uncles

As siblings of both of the parents, aunts and uncles (tíos) are
related to by their nieces and nephews (sobrinos) in a way that is
similar to the relationship between parents and children, illustrating
the generational characteristic that is present in relationships. Thus,
in the squatter settlements tíos are often treated as distant parents.
Pivotal to the option for a relatively close tie beween tíos and sobrinos
is the strength of solidarity that exists between ego's parents and their
siblings.

The following examples illustrate the way in which both the
generational aspects and merging of parental and parental siblings'
functions are evident in the tíos/sobrinos relationship. In the squatter
settlements parents' siblings are often expected to step into the parental
role during the absence of a parent. Parents' siblings may also bring
their sobrinos treats or take them to a movie or the circus on holidays.
Lola said in reference to her sobrinos, "I must have a special affection
for my sister's children, since they are almost like my own." An unmarried woman or particularly one who is married and yet remains childless may develop a close relationship to her sister's children. Often
it is the aunt or uncle who chooses the name for a newborn infant.
An aunt or uncle may also sponsor the baptism or the first hair-cutting
of the child, becoming its *padrino* or *madrina* (godfather or godmother),
thus making the guardian relationship more formal. In return, sobrinos
are expected to show tíos respect, to follow their commands, and to aid
them when necessary, just as they would treat their parents. Because
of the generally close relationship among siblings and traditional
clustering of siblings in Ciudadela Chalaca, children tend to grow up
in close proximity to their parents' siblings and to interact with them
daily.

PARIENTES CERCANOS AND PARIENTES LEJANOS

Beyond the range of familia in the model of kinship are the parientes cercanos, or near kinsmen. This group includes all cousins beyond first, second, and sometimes third cousins. Some informants included third cousins in familia; others put them in parientes cercanos. The reason for this difference may be related to regional highland differences in treatment of kin, or it may have some completely different explanation. This different interpretation of the placement of third cousins did not, however, cause a great deal of concern for informants, in contrast to anxiety expressed as to the placement of siblings. Third cousins are far enough from ego to comfortably be given a diffuse classification. Also included are those kinsmen termed *tíos* and *tías* but who are more distant than those tíos found in la familia, and those sobrinas and sobrinos who are not included in la familia. All parientes cercanos have well-defined links to ego, in contrast to parientes lejanos, who are often linked in a diffuse manner. Relationships with these kin in terms of expectations and obligations are similar to those found within the familia range. However, interaction is less frequent and the binding between these kin is more attentuated. Parientes cercanos are relatives with whom ego has an acknowledged and recognized kin tie and yet with whom interaction is not necessarily on a daily basis. Parientes cercanos are, however, those kin who are expected to participate fully in events such as wakes and weddings. In Ciudadela Chalaca, but not necessarily in Dulanto, they may be residentially clustered.

The range of parientes lejanos (distant kin) includes all remaining kin whom ego recognizes as kin but whose connecting links to ego are not necessarily clearly known. Ego may recognize a particular individual as a pariente lejano either because ego's parents considered this individual a relative or because of a shared apellido, which indicates that in some way they must be related. As with parientes cercanos, parientes lejanos, within the setting of the squatter settlement, may live in close proximity, in which case interaction may be relatively frequent. Parientes lejanos are expected to attend important family functions such as weddings and wakes and to collaborate with ego when closer kin are lacking.

PAISANOS

Beyond the rank of parientes lejanos is the large and very diffuse category termed *paisanos*, which in its most precise and least inclusive form includes all of those residents of the squatter settlement who have migrated from the same district in the highlands. More generally, the term *paisano* may refer to all of those from the same province or department or even to all highlanders in contrast to those born on the coast. Within the squatter settlements the paisano grouping generally is understood in the more restricted sense and is the basis for much of the traditional residential clustering. In Dulanto, because of the general residential dispersion, residents still identify with other paisanos, yet much of the cohesive activity found in Ciudadela Chalaca is absent. In Ciudadela Chalaca prior to the remodeling the paisano grouping was also commonly the grouping that participated in large-scale communal activities, such as the construction of a water spigot or of a chapel of the patron saint of the home village. As a last resort, one may always rely on one's paisanos for economic and emotional support if the complement of closer kin is inadequate. It is within the paisano grouping that one will most likely find confidants and supporters in political and community-wide activities. For example, children who attend primary and secondary schools located outside the squatter settlement feel more secure in the absence of kin if there are at least paisanos in their classes. In the marketplace and in public areas paisanos from the same highland district gravitate toward one another and tend to converse readily with one another. For example, Juana commented that when she and her husband and three small children attend a public gathering, such as a dance exhibit at the coliseum, they look for others who seem to be paisanos from their district of Huancayo, and they feel more comfortable sitting and perhaps conversing with their paisanos. It is within the paisano grouping that parents in the squatter settlements hope their children will marry.

Beyond the paisanos are those who do not figure in the scheme of kin relations. Among los otros, as contrasted with nosotros, the level of trust and social interaction drops sharply. Relationships are extended beyond the paisano range through the formation of alliances (see Chapter 8).

AFFINES

Where do affines fit into the model of concentric circles? In the squatter settlements, because the household is the basic economic unit, affines have special rights and duties within the household as well as during certain kin and paisano events. Except for occasional inclusion of spouses, affines were not generally included in the concentric-circle model provided by the residents of Ciudadela Chalaca and Dulanto. After all, it was explained, affines are not familia or parientes, they are something different. *Cuñado* (or *cuñada*) is a term which includes spouse's siblings and also ego's siblings' spouses; it also may be used to refer to "in-laws" in a general sense. The kinsmen of ego's spouse who are beyond the range of familia most generally are referred to as *parientes de mi esposo(a)* (my husband's [or wife's] relatives), while those affines within the familia and tied to one through a spouse are more commonly referred to as *cuñados*. Likewise, spouses of one's siblings are referred to as *cuñados*. Spouses of parent's siblings are tíos, but spouses of cousins and all parientes are generally given descriptive designations such as *esposo de mi prima* (my cousin's husband). The term *cuñado* denotes a closer relationship than a descriptive means of designation. The term *con-cuñado* refers to ego's spouse's sibling's spouse or to ego's sibling's spouse's sibling and is most commonly used by men or women who are married to spouses who are siblings to one another. With the common settling of siblings near one another in a squatter settlement such as Ciudadela Chalaca, con-cuñados frequently find themselves interacting on a daily basis as well as jointly aiding in large-scale celebrations such as sponsorship of fiestas in which their spouses (who are siblings) have an obligation. Often cuñados or con-cuñados are not only affines but also kinsmen or paisanos to one another. This potential for the opportunity to hold multiple statuses creates additional complexities in relationships.

Although there is frequent reference to the desirability for cuñados to cooperate and get along, there also often exists the potential for hostility between cuñados. The uneasy truce and the ambivalence often expressed toward cuñados may be an expression of the general ambivalence felt regarding the pull of obligations between one's siblings and one's family of procreation. Counteracting the tendency toward friction between cuñados, bonds of fictive kin are frequently formed in order to enhance trust, respect, and the ability to cooperate. A joking relationship that functions to ease tensions frequently develops between cuñados. Significantly enough, the jokes often entail mock pickpocketing or hiding objects from a cuñado. While these jokes are accepted with good humor among cuñados and provide a source of entertainment for other household members, there is a general acknowledgement that this form of joking contains subtle cues as to the potential economic rivalry that may exist between cuñados.

CHILDREN

CHAPTER 7

For a familia de la casa to be considered complete, the presence of children is of great importance. In the few instances in which natural children are not present, a couple generally arranges to raise one or more children of a sibling. This strategy is seen as advantageous for both families: the childless family will have a child who will both provide help and complete the family unit, while the family with perhaps too many children to care for easily is relieved of the responsibility of at least one child. In the city raising many children is no longer a desired goal. Many informants, both men and women, pointed out that a large number of children was considered an asset in the rural setting because they provided labor for agricultural tasks and created a "strong" family. However, in the city many believe that ideally the number of children should be four, perhaps five, and at the most six, pointing out that with more children, it is nearly impossible to feed them all, to say nothing of sending them to school. A study carried out in the squatter settlements of El Agustino indicates that the ideal number of children there is 3.8, yet the average number of births for

While a large number of children is considered an
asset in a rural setting, many residents of the city
believe that for them the ideal number of children per
family should be four, perhaps five, but six at the
most.

women 45 to 49 years old is 6.73 (Oficina Nacional de Estadística y
Censos 1969:44, 67).

As with many matters the general attitude of highland migrants
living in the squatter settlements is marked by practicality. Although
many residents profess Catholicism, religious training in the official
church doctrine is not rigorous, nor is attendance at official church
services in which a priest presides seen as a particularly important
aspect of one's life. The practicing of birth control is not viewed by
the migrant families as a moral question but as a practical one. Referred

to as *cuidandose* (taking care of oneself), birth control is discussed openly and frequently by many women along with other questions of health. The general feeling is that living in the city is expensive, and, if the family is to survive and attain material goals and upward mobility, then the number of children must be reduced.

At the other extreme, families with only one or two children are generally considered to be pitiful, not because the parents will not have the support of their children in their old age or the joy of many children making the household happy, but most consistently because, "It is sad if one does not have many brothers and sisters" or, "The children will be so lonely to be so few," or "They will be all alone and won't be able to help one another." It is the bond between siblings that is seen as fundamental to one's emotional and material well-being.

BIRTH AND INFANCY

During pregnancy most women of highland origin carry out their daily schedules as usual, including the continuation of often heavy manual labor, for it is believed that if one's muscles are strong from strenuous work childbirth will be easy. No special clothing is purchased for pregnancy; the everyday full skirts are just hitched a bit higher. In the last few months of pregnancy some women curtail their appearance in public and do not travel in crowded public buses because they find their *barrigas* (bellies) embarrassing or have difficulties with the fast pace of crowds on the public thoroughfares outside the squatter settlements. Other women express no qualms about continuing all public activities until the day of birth.

During the later months of pregnancy there is some discussion among the pregnant woman and her kin as to the probable and desired sex of the expected child. Some families at some stages of their developmental cycle prefer boys, others girls. Some mention is made that it is desirable that the first-born be a boy. However, it is also maintained that men like to have girl children and are often closest to their girls, while women like to have boys. Other women maintain that girls are desirable too since they will be a help in the home chores and will also provide more companionship. One woman remarked ruefully after the birth of her fourth male child in a row, "*Un otro sinvergüenza por el mundo*" ("Another tramp comes into the world").

In the metropolitan Lima area there are a number of public maternity hospitals which provide childbirth services; in 1974 the cost was five to six hundred soles. This minimum payment could be reduced if the family was completely without means. There also exist a number of private clinics which are believed to provide better care but charge more than the public hospitals. The advantages and disadvantages of going to a maternity hospital are often discussed, for this is the place where most of the women from Ciudadela Chalaca or Dulanto who decide to have their babies in a hospital can afford to go. There is first the problem of the expense of going to the maternity hospital, which is not inconsequential for a family in which daily earnings may not be much more then one hundred soles. Additionally, there may be expenses for medicine. There are also expressions of concern as to the real merits of hospital delivery compared to home delivery.

A number of women whose babies were delivered in the maternity hospital said that they were treated well by doctors who seemed to be dedicated and skillful. However, again and again the cruelty and neglect of the obstetric nurses who oversee the majority of the birth process was angrily mentioned. Some women said that they would never return to the maternity hospital because the nurses yelled and cursed at them, slapped them in the face, and pressed them too hard in the stomach. The women living in Ciudadela Chalaca and Dulanto said that during labor a woman should be cared for with gentle understanding and respect and certainly not with the disdain with which the obstetric nurses treat them. One woman recounted what was said to be a common experience, that after giving birth in the maternity hospital she was left on a very cold bed without even one blanket and that she shivered so much the entire bed shook. During a home delivery great care is taken to warm the new mother and infant immediately following birth.

Many women deliver their babies in their homes in the squatter settlement attended by the local midwives, who charge about thirty soles. Close kin often come to the house during childbirth to sit with the mother or visit her briefly. The father and other close male relatives are not excluded; however, they tend to stay in the background, leaving the care of the mother to the midwife. Pain-relievers are often purchased from the local pharmacy; the woman in labor drinks herb tea, and gentle massages are given to her arms and legs and abdomen. She is encouraged to walk as much as possible.

Some women prefer to spend a few weeks in the house resting, while others begin their round of duties less than a week after giving birth. As Celsa said, "It is difficult, especially when there are many children, to stay in bed. So I just get up as soon as I can." Rags used for diapers are tied loosely around the baby's waist and between its legs. The infant is often swaddled tightly in clothes and slung on his mother's back in a woven cloth in the fashion found in the highlands.

Almost all of the women breastfeed their infants, saying that breast milk is what makes a baby fat and healthy. A few of the very young mothers, particularly those in their late teens who were born in the squatter settlements, have tried using baby bottles in the manner that is popular with the urban middle class. The few who have tried bottles find them an extra expense and bother; as one young mother said, "And for what, that I don't have already?" Thus the general consensus is that breastfeeding an infant is best. Breastfeeding may continue until the baby is two years old or until the beginning of the next pregnancy, whichever comes first. Among most women there is no modesty associated with breastfeeding in public. However, those women who are more aware of middle-class mores may not nurse in public. A baby carried on his mother's back is given the breast whenever he begins to cry. Such an infant is generally quiet and relaxed, presenting only a small lump on his mother's back as she goes about her work.

After the baby is weaned, a good deal of the responsibility for the young child is placed in the hands of an older, at times only slightly older, sibling. Most often, it is an older sister who cares for the young child. So begins the lifelong close association among siblings, each sibling having cared for a younger one during the period of transition between completely dependent infancy and relatively independent childhood.

CHILDHOOD

When families are large, a number of siblings often share one bed, sleeping head to foot either lengthwise or crosswise. Most people do not change into night clothing but may shed an outer layer of clothing before retiring. In the morning it is often the older siblings who dress the smallest child and are responsible for washing his hands and face and combing his hair. Both parents or other adults who may be in the house oversee and coordinate these activities; however, it is the older siblings who carry out most of the actual interaction with the smaller siblings. By the age of four or five most children have a younger sibling who is his or her responsibility. Likewise, it is the oldest brother or sister who has the working responsibility for all younger siblings delegated to him or her by the parents. Once the child is weaned, parents speak of their concern for him in terms of

An infant is often swaddled tightly in clothes and slung on his
mother's back in a woven cloth until he is old enough to walk.

providing food, clothing, educational expenses, and contact with influential individuals who will aid him in the future. Expressed parental concern does not center on providing emotional security or companionship for the children. In the day-to-day reality of interaction the parents act primarily as workers who provide for the children economically and as coordinators of the children's activities; the children's physical contact, direct interaction, and companionship grows out of the sibling solidarity that even by the age of three or four is strongly developed.

From a very early age children learn to interact with other children of all ages. It is within these non-age-segregated childhood groups that they learn much of the interactional patterns which are used in adulthood. The most common playmates are siblings, cousins, or paisanos. Until the age of five or six and before they have begun school, children tend to play in sexually undifferentiated groups, and the games they play are not especially associated with one sex or another. At about the age of five or six, children form groups differentiated by sex, the only exception being that a child who may have the responsibility of caring for a younger sibling of a different sex will include him or her in the play group. Although there is no avoidance or rivalry between groups of male and female playmates, there is a divergence of interests and types of games which are played.

The division of playmates by sex is further accentuated at the time school is begun. The schools which are attended by the children living in Ciudadela Chalaca run on morning and afternoon sessions, with boys attending one and girls attending the other. Thus, once children reach school age, the absence of the other sex both in and out of school is a deterrent for the formation of sexually integrated groups of playmates. In Dulanto, however, where one of the schools is participating in an educational reform policy, classrooms contain both boys and girls, thus allowing for some interaction between the sexes.

The games that children in Ciudadela Chalaca play rarely require traditional toys, nor does each child in a family have a number of toys which he considers his own. A family may have a doll, a ball, or a toy truck nailed together from rough lumber, but these toys are not the exclusive property of any one child and most often are shared without qualms or possessiveness among the children in the family. This focus on sharing the few toys owned by a family is another indication of the feeling of solidarity that exists among the sibling group. The lack of preconstructed toys forces the children, like their parents, to exercise ingenuity in using the materials at hand to fulfill their needs. With small sticks, rocks, and lines drawn in the soil, children create miniature versions of the world around them. From the point of view of many children, the squatter settlement, with its numerous intriguing passageways and buildings on which to climb, fulfills the function of a vast jungle gym and playground.

The stress of childhood play is upon social relationships, a childhood counterpart of the adult emphasis placed on social interaction. Most play activity entails interaction with others; lone play is not encouraged in children. The children's play usually consists of make-believe or imitation of adult activity.

Lest the impression be given that children spend the day at play, it should be stressed that free play times for children are usually short periods snatched between fulfilling multiple family obligations. In spite of the common reference by parents to their sacrifice and concern for their children and their future, the nuclear family of procreation is not child-centered, nor are children given a great deal of tolerance. Each child *must* fulfill his or her obligation to the other family members, and, if he fails to do so, punishment is generally sure and often painful lashes on the back or legs from the braided whip which hangs prominently in the house. Both girls and boys are whipped when necessary; however, most parents agree that boys tend to be harder to handle than girls. Punishment is severe and short-lived, and parents do not continue to loom over their children as stern authority figures after the occasional whipping has been meted out. Parents expect each child to fulfill his or her family obligations, to work hard, and to share the burden of family life. However, once this attitude is impressed on the child, the relationship between parents and children is generally nonauthoritarian.

Besides caring for younger siblings, children generally have daily chores which consist of tending the animals that the family raises or carrying pails of water from the public spigot. Even a small child can fulfill the duty of picking through the raw rice each day to remove small rocks and impurities. Women who work in the market often use their small children as assistants to weigh produce or tend the stall for short periods of time. A child who has attended a few years of school may be of considerable help in writing price tags and making change. In a home that has a small house-front store, a child may often wait on a customer or be in attendance to alert an adult should a customer appear. Children may also help on a general basis in family enterprises such as shoe repair, preparation of food to be sold in small carts, or collecting scrap lumber or metal. Once girls reach the age of nine or ten and are skillful enough to handle the rather dangerous kerosene burners on which most women cook, they too will help

Chores are a regular part of children's daily life.
The young girl here is carrying refuse to be dumped.

prepare the meals. Young girls also help with the clothes-washing, either at the public water spigots or with a bucket and scrubbing board at home.

Aside from the daily tasks which are expected of each child, there are many times during the day when, for a multitude of reasons, a child's services will be needed and a sharp command from the parent will be heard: "Irene, take the baby," "Nicanor, charge an onion at the store," or "Miriam, go see if your Aunt Lucilla has a needle." Children are the errand-runners who make the household's small daily purchases — one aspirin from the drugstore or a box of matches from the marketplace — or who are sent to borrow small items from a parent's sibling.

The role of messenger is also reserved for children. It is the children who function as the rapid network of communication among households which interact daily but which lack a telephone system. In the squatter settlements one commonly hears of *pasando la voz*, that is, "getting the word" to someone, and it is through speedy young messengers that this passing of useful information is carried out. It is the children who are told, "Go see if *Simplemente María* is on your aunt's TV yet," or, "Go look next door to see if Alejandro [an uncle] is home from work." This type of information is rarely passed beyond the limits of the paisano residential grouping unless a special *compadrazgo* relationship has been established.

Being accustomed to doing chores from an early age, children in their early teens and even younger carry out tasks that entail a good deal of responsibility. It is expected that they will comply with their obligations as a member of a family unit. Two or three teenaged sisters may, in addition to doing their schoolwork, take on almost the full household responsibilities of caring for younger siblings, purchasing and preparing food, and washing clothes if their mother has a particularly heavy work load as a vendor, is taking advantage of the opportunity for overtime work during the peak seasons in a fish cannery, or has to return to the highlands for some months to attend to the harvesting of a crop on property that she owns. Likewise, a young boy may often earn money after school as an apprentice in a family enterprise, in his own business such as shining shoes, or in a job such as collecting fares on a bus. All adults and all children are expected to carry through at the level of their capability in an industrious and productive manner. Each individual is viewed as a responsible member of a kin grouping with a variety of obligations which must be fulfilled in order to remain in good standing.

Within the nuclear family of procreation, children who are siblings demonstrate a strong sense of unity and a warm affection for one another. Siblings will often "accompany" one another when sent on an errand by a parent. Siblings may also present a block against a parent. For example, if a parent threatens to whip a child, the other children will often plead in their sibling's defense. Overt sibling rivalry is rarely manifested and when it is, adults are quick to chastise any child who engages in such behavior. This notable lack of rivalry is replaced in most cases by a sentiment of protective solidarity.

In families in which the childen have followed in close succession, usually at two-year intervals, there is no traditional pattern of resentment of the new baby by the one just replaced at the mother's breast, as is reported in other Latin American countries. The older child at two or two-and-a-half is usually just at the age of weaning and is being shifted from the primary care of the mother to that of an older sibling. Evidently this incorporation into the world of children and away from that of the mother offers enough compensations and rewards to forestall any jealousy toward the newborn sibling.

BIRTH ORDER OF SIBLINGS

Central to the functioning of the sibling group among both children and adults is a hierarchy among siblings that is based on birth order. As mentioned previously, the child-care pattern in which an older sibling is responsible during much of the day for a younger sibling establishes a protective/dependency relationship among siblings which links all of the siblings from the oldest to the youngest. While one's relationship to one's elder sibling is one of dependency, it is one of protectiveness to the younger sibling. The system is only asymmetrical at the ends: the youngest sibling has no one within the nuclear family toward whom to be protective and the eldest sibling must depend upon himself or the parents for protection. However, in practice, because of the generally close relationship among first cousins and other kin of the same generation, the hierarchy based on age extends in many respects beyond the nuclear family. A youngest child will most likely have an even younger cousin whom he may protect.

Parents and most adults treat an eldest child, whether a boy or a girl, with special attention and care. The eldest child also has unique responsibilities and prerogatives. The parents generally speak of this first-born child with an affection not often found for the subsequent children, except perhaps for the youngest child when he is still quite young. The eldest child is often given a nickname of endearment by the parents. It is this child for whom the parents especially hope to find upper-status, influential godparents; it is the eldest child for whom the greatest concern is expressed regarding the people with whom he or she interacts and the ultimate choice in a marriage partner. Often in the squatter settlements the parents' plans for the eldest child's future are the most spectacular. Educationally, the oldest child's progress in school is avidly watched by the parents, who praise his or her industriousness and intelligence in the presence of the other children in the hopes that the oldest will provide a model worthy of emulation by the other children.

Within each nuclear family the ranked hierarchy is based on sibling birth order, with the mother and father usually viewed as exercising equal dominance in relation to the children. Entire nuclear families are also ranked according to the sibling birth order of the

All siblings from oldest to youngest are linked in a child-care pattern in which an older sibling is responsible during much of the day for a younger sibling. Here a six-year-old carries her baby brother on her back in a manta.

adults who head them. This is the same ranked hierarchy which has continued since the childhood of these individuals, who as adults also have their families of procreation. It is the oldest adult sibling of six who says, "I must keep the family together. We are all the same, and in the end I would do anything for my brothers and sisters." María expressed the sentiment of many when she said, "Although I love my children and worry about them and their future and know that it is my responsibility to fight for them every day, I think that I am really closer to my brothers and sisters in many ways than to my own children. Maybe it is just because they [my siblings] are also adults I can talk to. Who knows?"

Unless there is some personality characteristic of an eldest sibling which prevents him or her from carrying out the expected role of sibling leader, the family of procreation of the eldest sibling within a group of siblings represents the hub of stability for other siblings and their families. Often it is the eldest sibling and his or her family who have migrated first from the highlands to the coast. In the general absence of the parents of adult migrants in the coastal squatter settlements, the eldest sibling additionally takes on the responsibilities of maintaining the cohesion and solidarity of the sibling group. For example, Ernestina felt that her husband Agrapino, thirty-two, was beginning to drink too much, so that he was not carrying the family responsibilities as he should. Her criticism met with no response or improvement. She then went to talk to Agrapino's eldest brother, Sebastián. The next time that Agrapino came home drunk, Ernestina surreptitiously sent her daughter to fetch Sebastián, who came into Agrapino's house and whipped him with the braided rawhide whip meant for discipline of children. Sebastián spoke fiercely to Agrapino about the disgrace he was causing to his kin and the suffering he was bringing to his wife and children. Agrapino wept. A week later Ernestina reported that Agrapino had vowed to mend his ways and was not drinking. Acting as disciplinarian is viewed in the squatter settlements as a necessary and expected aspect of the role of the eldest sibling.

Among a group of adult siblings and their families of procreation living in the squatter settlement, there is contact and some interaction with the parents who have remained in the highlands. Often it is the control or ownership of land in the highlands that is the last thread of power held by elderly parents. And often it is only this land and its future inheritance by the children which draws comment and concern about the parents from the adult children now living in the city. Josefina expressed the following straightforward sentiment in regard to her widowed mother: "She always comes to visit us each year, but we [Josefina and her siblings] think she should come to live here with us. Now only my youngest sister is there in the highlands to take care of her. That's not right. We should all take care of her, so when she dies, we'll all divide her land."

In the squatter settlements it is generally the eldest sibling who wields the ultimate authority and who makes most important decisions. What will happen when the youth of the squatter settlements become middle-aged parents and an elderly parental generation is actually present in the city is unclear. The fact that the elderly parental generation has remained in the highlands has strengthened the position of the eldest sibling and enhanced sibling solidarity in the squatter settlements.

Among sibling groups vis-à-vis their primos hermanos a hierarchy based on the birth order exists. Thus the eldest sibling who is also the eldest of all of his father's or mother's siblings' children who are in the city plays a particularly dominant role regarding the solidarity and interaction of all of these children. For example, Susana, who is eleven, plays a dominant role in her relationship with her prima hermana Obaldina, who is five. However, Obaldina's eldest sister, eighteen, is clearly the leader of the two sets of siblings since Susana's eldest brother is only fifteen. Thus age plays an important role in the interaction of sets of siblings. Among adults the eldest of a group of siblings and first cousins takes on the responsibilities of organizing cooperative efforts. For example, it is Leoncio, the eldest sibling and the eldest of the primos hermanos in the city, who coordinates the backing of his mother's sponsorship of the patron saint fiesta in their highland home town. From each of six siblings he obtained 5,000 soles and from primos hermanos he obtained the loan of equipment and the contributions of food and skills such as dressmaking, butchering, and food preparation. The same role is evident among the young people of the squatter settlements, although their goals are often nontraditional. For example, it is the eldest sibling and the eldest first cousin who organized and coordinated the activities associated with a younger cousin's birthday party. It is the eldest sibling and the eldest first cousin who organizes and is consistently elected president of the paisano-based soccer team. Also, it is an oldest sibling and oldest cousin who at twenty-three organized and became the lead singer for a Latino rock band which includes his two siblings, three first cousins, and a brother-in-law. Thus it is expected of the eldest sibling that his or her leadership prerogative will be exercised.

FORMATION OF ALLIANCES

CHAPTER 8

In the initially alien environment of the city the migrant must rely first on the network of kin who have come from the same rural area, later putting into play the option of extending this network to non-kin through the formation of alliances. Affiliation with many individuals is not seen by the migrants only or even primarily as a means to wealth and prestige but as a necessary end in itself. An individual with numerous kin and paisanos as well as extensive and well-maintained alliances is perceived by the migrants as being well on his or her way to power and prestige and able to adapt readily to the exigencies of urban living. Alliances are also formed in order to reinforce existing relationships for activation in the city.

Many of the basic structural characteristics and functions found within the ego-centered network of a kindred are also found in the network of alliances. These similarities are clear to the migrant families living in the coastal squatter settlements, and the basic strategy which is so fundamental to a consideration of one's circle of kin is also carried out during the process of alliance formation. In the squatter settlements ego is central to his individual network of alliances in the same structural sense that he is central to a kindred. The most important feature of established ties is reciprocal obligation, which is expressed in multiple forms. Not only are the characteristics of ego's network of alliances similar to those found in kin ties based on the kindred, but there is often an actual overlap of the kin tie and the alliance tie. Thus ego's kinsmen may also often be tied to him through additional multiple, formal alliances. Because the formation of alliances, especially marriage and *compadrazgo* alliances, is a basic strategy of the highland communities, what is found in the coastal squatter settlement shares many traditional forms with the highlands, but is often adapted to urban needs and is carried out through urban means.

The urban setting and even the high population density of the squatter settlements are viewed positively by the residents. This positive evaluation is particularly evident in regard to opportunities for the formation and maintenance of alliances. In contrast to the residents of the relatively small and often isolated highland villages, many individuals in the city are able to extend their alliances numerically and include a variety of social levels in ways never possible in the highlands.

After simple survival in the city, the generalized goal of most of the migrant families is to become urbanites, an objective which includes, but does not necessarily stop at, home ownership, a steady job, and children who are moving into the middle class. Many of these goals are achieved through relationships which have been initiated through formal alliances. Each person aspires to broaden his network of alliances to include individuals in a variety of social positions so that, should the occasion arise, the reciprocal obligation in his favor may be activated. An individual who has an extensive network of alliances is admired both for his control of potential resources and for his skill in manipulating a valuable social asset.

The emphasis which is placed on networks of alliance as opposed to corporate groups makes disassembly and then reconstitution of a personal network, with additions or subtractions, feasible during the migration and adaptation process. The mechanisms for creating formal alliances are brought from the highlands and are mutually understood by all of the migrants. As long as the jointly held values and culturally defined rules of alliance formation are carried to the city by each person, the eventual construction of a large personal network of alliances is workable.

Migrant residents of the squatter settlements see themselves as living in an open social system in which upward mobility is a definite possibility. There exists a firm belief that with hard work, diligence, and careful planning, one may enter the established middle class in spite of rural highland origins. To many people living in Ciudadela Chalaca and Dulanto, migration itself is considered an event that acts to free one from the relatively closed highland system in which upward mobility is viewed as virtually impossible. Indeed, the contrast between the living conditions in the rural highlands and the urban squatter settlements is great, and, by the standards of the migrants, this change is viewed as upward mobility. The migrants' general enthusiasm and optimism regarding their escape from their past and their future potential for upward mobility is a pervasive sentiment in the squatter settlements.

CHOOSING A SPOUSE

Marriage activates the most vital types of reciprocal relationships that are found in the squatter settlements. It opens a bridge of interaction between two groups which previously had neither the desire for interaction nor the trust to carry it out. The affines acquired through marriage broaden one's options in that the network of individuals whom one may refer to as "my kin" (even though they are only affines) is expanded tremendously. It is through affines, for example, that a person may seek influential allies when he needs a job, a word in the right place during court litigation, or a letter of recommendation for a son who would like to join the merchant marines. These needs may be small details of existence, but it is through personalized contact that they are effected and an individual of highland origin is able to function successfully in the city. Although affines may be approached gingerly for this sort of request and with a full knowledge that the obligation must be reciprocated at some time in the future, an extensive network of affines on good terms significantly expands the number of those upon whom one may rely for aid.

The residents of the squatter settlements who have come from the highlands are quite consistently in agreement as to marriage proscriptions that must be carefully observed. As previously mentioned, one may not marry within la familia, and ego's spouse may not share the same apellido as ego. For example, Filipe Pantoja (apellido from father) Rojas (apellido from mother) may not marry anyone with the apellidos Pantoja or Rojas. However, his mother's maternal apellido, Serna, which Filipe does not have, will allow him to marry someone with the apellido Serna as long as this individual is not within the rank of familia.

Whereas the apellidos passed from males to female descendants are carried by male and female grandchildren, they do not continue past this link. Thus, female-linked apellidos are lost within at least two generations, while male-linked apellidos remain indefinitely. Thus, the apellidos carried through the males maintain stronger proscriptive weight in contrast to those apellidos obtained from a female ascendent relative. In addition, marriage is prohibited between compadres in which a respect relationship is the norm.

What are the explanations for these proscriptions? Residents of the squatter settlements commented that marriage should not be carried out within a familia or among those with the same apellidos because "this creates problems within the families. There are always disagreements such as about inheritance," or "such marriages can bring disasters." Also, "the children of such marriages are never right; either they don't think right or there is something physically wrong with them." Solamina reported that in her home village in Apurimac such an incestuous couple would be driven out because of the villagers' fear that their presence would bring danger to everyone. One such couple within a familia escaped to Lima, where they lived for a time in a squatter settlement. "No one seems to care here quite so much. Though perhaps only because it's not known that they are cousins." In the squatter settlement the general and common accusation between various antagonistic paisano groupings is: "They are not like us. There is something twisted about these people. It is rumored that there is incest and that their marriages are very bad." Marriages which might seem to be "too close" are justified again and again through a careful explanation of kin links, often involving half-siblings, in order to prove that the marriage is respectable and not stigmatized by the moral repugnance of an incestuous union. The stringency of this prohibition was demonstrated in 1974 when a young woman living in Ciudadela Chalaca was forbidden by her family to marry her boyfriend primarily because the boyfriend's maternal apellido was the same as the young woman's paternal apellido, even though it was highly unlikely that there was in reality any kin link, since the two families had come from geographically distant areas of the highlands.

Much of the negative gossip that abounds in the squatter settlements centers on the possibility of incestuous unions within certain paisano or family groupings. Such gossip is often an effective social weapon in undermining the prestige and moral credibility of a family. For example, Ana said that one of her distant cousins, of whom she was not very fond, had married her primo hermano. Both marriage partners had come from a highland village which was very isolated and in which it was rumored that the marriage of primos hermanos had occurred before. Their only child was born mentally retarded, a fact which Ana interpreted as her cousin's *castigo* (punishment) for having married a primo hermano. Likewise, the birth of physically deformed children may be interpreted as resulting from marriages that were too close. In reference to a girl with a cleft palate, a non-paisano neighbor said, "Her parents are some kind of close cousins even though they won't admit it, and that is why the girl is the way she is."

Sexual relations within the familia are particularly repugnant, and waves of gossip that bring considerable shame to a family spread through the squatter settlements from time to time regarding incestuous acts between, for example, half-siblings or an uncle and niece. In such a situation, whether the gossip is true or not, the family is generally forced to separate the supposed offending parties by having an older brother join the army or a visiting uncle move to another household. Sexual relations between affines are viewed as almost as disgraceful as between consanguines who are too close. Gossip abounds regarding some stepfathers and their teenage stepdaughters. Numerous jokes and specific references exist regarding the proverbial niece of a married woman who comes to Lima from the highlands to stay with her aunt in order to study in secondary school, but who subsequently learns more about life from her aunt's husband than in school. Thus marriage proscriptions and the ever-present potential for incest are of common concern, even anxiety, in the squatter settlements.

Whom, then, should one marry? What are the marriage prescriptions in the squatter settlements? First, it is preferred by the adults that their children marry paisanos, that is, those who are from the same highland district or whose parents have come from the same district. There are, however, varying degrees of preferential marriage. If one does not marry a paisano, then a spouse should preferably be at least someone from the same highland department. As distance between the highland origins of the prospective spouses increases, so does family discomfort over an impending match. However, the least preferred category of marriage partners for the highlanders are the costeños, especially zambos. As Domatilda, whose oldest son is seventeen, comments, "My son knows that the girls from the highlands will respect their husbands and they will not go off with another man. And they work hard. Not like the girls from the coast who are not taught anything."

Some people express the rationale for marriage preference culturally, as Domatilda does, and some, racially. When Hernán heard that one of his nieces had been associating with a zambo, his comment was, "The next disgrace she'll bring to the family will be to give us a *zambito*." In 1974, when Eva married a young man whose parents had migrated from a different department than her parents, her mother Marcelina said, "Even though his family is not one of us and that may cause some problems for them, I am just glad that she did not marry one of those lazy costeños." Isbell (1973:206) found a similar tendency in another squatter settlement. Of 55 households, all but 18 marriages were of co-villagers. Of these 18 marriages, 5 were between people from the same district or province and the other 13 were between highlanders.

The second marriage prescription is that once a sibling or close kinsman such as an uncle or aunt has married into a congenial family, then it is desirable for younger siblings or close kin to follow suit. This second marriage preference creates the common and desired pattern of multiple binding alliances between families. Because sets of siblings living in the squatter settlements are generally large and very often include numerous half-siblings, the possibilities of complex alliances are multiple when traced across a few generations.

In the type of preferential marriage in which sets of siblings tend to marry close kin of another family there is created a situation in which the tie among siblings is strengthened, thereby providing for more constant interaction and more assurance of residential proximity of siblings who are often able to interact as a unit. For example, José, who is from Apurimac, is the eldest sibling and the first one to come to Lima. He has four siblings also in Lima and two younger ones who are still in the highlands. His family of orientation has very little land in the highlands but is viewed as fortunate, since five of the adult children have steady jobs on the coast. José met and married Florinda on the coast nineteen years ago. Her family owns a comparatively large amount of land in a highland village which is one hour's walk from José's home village. By 1974 two of José's younger brothers were married to nieces of Florinda and a third brother was married to her cousin. José says, "It is very important when there is a sense of understanding among siblings. When there is confidence between people, then they are able to work together. This is particularly good in my family since we can all come and go in one another's houses and rely on one another. If a problem comes up, we can all face it together."

In spite of the economic and domestic functions of the nuclear family of procreation, it is the family of orientation, and especially the sibling unit within the squatter settlement, to which each individual feels a great deal of emotional attachment and in which certain vital reciprocal obligations are carried out. The resulting ambiguity of allegiance between the family of procreation and the family of orientation is found in the model of concentric circles (see Fig. 6.1), in which many people expressed hesitancy and real concern as to whether siblings should be considered part of the familia de la casa which emotionally they seem to be, or whether they should be placed in the familia, since they do not live in the same household. For example, Nicanor pondered whether he would use his savings to aid his brother in sponsoring a fiesta or to buy his family of procreation a new radio. He helped his brother. Justina fantasized that should she obtain a job in the United States, she would then save money to bring either her sister or her husband to join her. She could not decide between them. Although the dilemma of allegiance varies in intensity from individual to individual and is handled in various ways in the face of each unique situation, the dilemma itself is an area of concern for many residents of the squatter settlements. Preferential marriage between the members of the families already joined by marriage somewhat diminishes this conflict. When one's siblings or at least primos hermanos or even nieces or nephews are married to one's spouse's close kin, the needs and obligations of both kin groups frequently coincide. That is, in working for the good of oneself as a member of a sibling unit, one may also be working for the good of one's spouse's siblings and close kin. The effects of this strategy are often seen graphically in reciprocal house construction, in which a group of siblings and first cousins who rotate in helping to construct one another's houses are also often helping to construct the houses of their spouses' kin.

The following comments by Tito is illustrative of the extent to which the choice of a spouse is consciously linked to considerations regarding siblings and other members of the family of orientation.

> Before I married Obaldina, I had another *compañera*. Her family was nice to me and I liked her. But I knew that (because she was not a *paisano*) if we stayed together, little by little I would become more and more distant from my brothers and sisters. Although she kept coming to look for me I decided to find someone who would fit into the family better.

In those families in which marriages have not followed the preferential form of marriage the dilemma of allegiance is worked out situationally, through a balancing act, trying to adequately appease obligations to both the spouse and children, and the near kin of orientation.

Because of the possibility of conflicting interests, there is a potential wariness among affines. The formal marriage ceremony may be alive both with latent hostility between the two groups of kin who will soon become affines and with multiple mechanisms to deflect and channel this hostility. The concern as to how affines, as well as the newlyweds, will get along is one of the basic foci of anxiety surrounding marriage. In families in which multiple marriage exchanges have occurred, there is less chance for divisive gossip to spread. Also, future affines are known and, ideally, trusted individuals.

In the squatter settlements both the adults and the youth express a strong concern with "romantic love," and the ultimate decision for the choice of a spouse is the prerogative of those considering marriage. However, parents still effect considerable influence, although in perhaps a less overt manner than was the case in the highlands. Young people may be lectured on the importance of marrying a paisano or at least another highlander. By the time most youths reach marriageable age, their enculturation has thoroughly stressed the positive character traits of paisanos in contrast to other populations in the squatter settlements. Parents are quite concerned that their children do not become involved with what they define as undesirable elements, particularly those costeños whom they suspect to be involved in illegal activities or prostitution. Most celebrations and social activities in which the initial stages of courtship frequently occur take place among groups of paisanos. Although there is some diversity in marriages and less parental control than in the highlands, there still exists a strong tendency in the squatter settlements to choose a spouse from among preferential categories.

Ideally, the newly married couple, either at the time of marriage or at least by the time children are born, establishes a home separate but not distant from that of the parents of both spouses. In Ciudadela Chalaca prior to the remodeling a newly married couple settled where it could find a place, if it could convince the community council that its claim to a lot was justified. Since the remodeling and the introduction of extensive and controlled qualifications for being awarded a lot, the potential for a newly married couple to establish a separate household has been greatly reduced. One of the most pressing problems of the relocation was the question of placing young couples who were living in the household of one of the parents. After much debate they were placed on the list of excedentes. However, a few young couples, particularly those married more than five years and with small children, did manage at the time of the relocation to obtain a lot either in Dulanto or, less commonly, in Ciudadela Chalaca.

When neolocality is not possible, the factors considered in making the choice of residence includes available space, willingness on the part of one set of parents to have the couple move in, and proximity to the couple's place of employment. In a marriage between non-paisanos, there is also the question of which of the spouses will leave the paisano cluster in which he or she has grown up. Commonly, a member of a well-united and strong sibling group who does not want to or cannot marry a member of a closely aligned family chooses an individual with weak family ties who will then move into the residential area of the stronger group. This pattern can affect either the man or the woman, but there is a slightly greater tendency for a woman to join her husband's group.

MARRIAGE

In the squatter settlements the concept of marriage covers a range of activities and events from informal living together as convivientes, to the more formalized civil marriage, to the religious marriage. In the squatter settlement of El Agustino the following breakdown was found (Oficina Nacional de Estadística y Censos 1969:21):

Single	16.2%
Married	52.5%
Civil marriage	17.1%
Religious marriage	11.0%
Civil and religious marriages	24.4%
Convivientes	25.4%
Separated	3.9%
Widowed	1.7%

Official figures tend to overreport marriage and underreport convivientes. There is a reluctance among many individuals in the squatter settlements to reveal that they are convivientes. This hesitation is primarily due not to a moral stigma but rather to the fact that only the more wealthy and powerful migrants are able to afford the cost of the bureaucratic red tape and the post-wedding festivities of a formal wedding ceremony. Direct questions as to marital status are considered indelicate at best and a cause for intense embarrassment at worst. However, since a formal marriage is usually recorded with a photograph which is prominently displayed in the house and the topic eventually enters casual conversation, an approximation of the numbers of those married may be obtained. In my sample of 85 heads of households in Ciudadela Chalaca and Dulanto in 1974, 25 couples were convivientes, 43 couples were married, the status of ten couples was unknown, and seven heads of households were single, widowed, or separated. These figures represent an increase over the number married in 1969: many couples who had been convivientes then felt they would have a better chance of obtaining a lot in Dulanto if they were formally married and so took advantage of one of the mass weddings organized at the time of the relocation.

The term *compromiso* is often used to refer to a person who is a conviviente. However, this term is also used in reference to a situation that is an intermittent and short-term affair in which joint housekeeping is not necessarily established. It is the rare couple which does not *convivir* (live together) before the official wedding has taken place. Similar arrangements of living together as they are traditionally practiced in the highlands have been described by Bolton (1972), Carter (1972), and Lambert (1972). To most of the migrant residents of the squatter settlements, this period of living together is viewed as a sensible measure which assures that the couple will "get used to one another" to some degree. Many couples live together as convivientes for years and raise numerous children before the timing is auspicious and resources have been accumulated for a formal ceremony and celebration.

Courtship

Among the youth in the squatter settlements social contact generally takes place in large groups of kin and paisanos. It is at birthday parties, wedding celebrations, and Sunday soccer and volleyball matches that young men and women get together most frequently. On these occasions develop close friendships which may eventually become conviviente arrangements or marriages.

Sexual relations prior to the formation of a long-term marriage relationship are generally viewed by parents as a part of the expected courtship pattern. However, considerable anxiety on the part of parents, particularly mothers, is expressed that a daughter may become pregnant before finding someone who will be a good marriage partner. Pregnancy outside of a marriage relationship is not morally stigmatic, but parents are concerned about the economic burden which a child may incur, especially for a young woman for whom they desire a secondary education and perhaps some technical training. However, in the squatter settlements, in contrast to the middle- and upper-class urban sectors of Lima, female virginity is not particularly valued. Sexual relations are generally viewed as a part of the process of becoming adult as well as an integral aspect of all normal human activity.

Although ideally a marriage, of either informal conviviente or legal contract status, is a lifelong commitment, it is the rare person who will not in his or her lifetime have more than one spouse. This tendency is the result of the high death rate; the frequent short-lived, youthful compromiso; and the strong belief that, because of the division of household tasks along sexual lines, men and women need to live together.

Cambio de Aros

In urban middle- and upper-class society, what is called the *cambio de aros* (exchange of rings) is a relatively simple engagement announcement and ceremony. Within the squatter settlements this urban tradition is gaining popularity and functions as a formal announcement for those who are convivientes and who may or may not at some point follow through with a civil or religiously recognized marriage. In the squatter settlements the cambio de aros is similar to a small-scale wedding but without the expense and time involved in a civil or religious wedding. On a modest scale the compromiso of the couple becomes a recognized social fact. Because the cambio de aros is an urban tradition, it is particularly attractive to the generation raised in the squatter settlements.

After Alfonso and Lucilla had lived together at his family's house in Ciudadela Chalaca for almost a year and a half, and were expecting a child within a few months, it was decided by both sets of parents and the couple that a party marking a cambio de aros was desirable. Engraved invitations were sent one week in advance to 85 households of paisanos and to some of the neighborhood friends of the couple. In this case, the preparation of food and the purchase of beer was shared by both sets of parents. The party was held in Alfonso's family's home, the living room of which was festooned with crepe paper. The furniture had been removed and, as is customary at parties held in a home, chairs lined the walls. By ten o'clock in the evening the guests began to arrive and stood in clusters around the room or seated themselves in chairs. A large group of the younger guests stood in groups on both sides of the doorway. Throughout the night the guests danced to recordings of both traditional highland huaynos and "modern" *cumbias* (Colombian dance popular among the teenagers).

At midnight the cambio de aros ceremony took place. A recording of the wedding march from Lohengrin was played, and Lucilla, wearing a pink satin dress and preceded by her cousin, entered the room. She carried a small bouquet. Alfonso stood in the living room between the man and woman who had been chosen previously as *padrino* and *madrina* (sponsors) for the couple. The padrino had worked with Alfonso's father at the docks for ten years and was a paisano but not a kinsman. The padrinos had purchased the rings for both Alfonso and Lucilla. Standing on either side of the padrinos were the parents of Alfonso and Lucilla. After Lucilla joined the semicircle, standing next to Alfonso, the padrino gave a short speech indicating that this simple ceremony should mark the beginning of a life together for the young couple and for both families. The padrino then placed a gold ring on the hand of Lucilla, while the madrina did the same for Alfonso. Then the young couple danced together to a waltz tune, followed by the padrinos, the parents of the couple, and the rest of the guests. Huaynos and cumbias were played and general dancing and festivities were begun. Small glasses of champagne were served to all present by the women in Alfonso's family. The men in both families served beer in a traditional and ritualized manner which involves toasts with each serving. Soon after the ceremony a spicy pork-and-potatoes dish, traditionally served at weddings, was served by Alfonso's mother and aunts to all the married guests. Dancing and toasting zestfully continued until three in the morning, when another dish of rice and sauce was served to all present. The dancing and toasting resumed until after dawn, when the guests — after some final lengthy toasts to Alfonso and Lucilla — began to return to their homes to catch a few hours of sleep.

Many of the features of this party, such as the dancing and toasting all night, are standard events at baptisms, birthday parties, weddings, and many other rites of passage. Each weekend in both Ciudadela Chalaca and Dulanto the sound of music and gay festivities overflows from numerous houses into the dusty streets.

The Civil Marriage

In Peru civil as well as religious marriages constitute legal marriage. A couple may choose either or both forms. The civil marriage has many legal advantages if a couple at some later date must deal with certain government matters. On the other hand, the religious marriage confers prestige and has numerous social advantages which accrue from setting in motion reciprocal obligations resulting from the elaborate festivities following the wedding ceremony. Families with the resources and the stamina necessary to thread through two sets of bureaucratic paperwork may choose both forms of marriage.

The civil ceremony brings recognition of the marriage by the state. Numerous documents, including the couple's birth certificates, voting cards, certificates of place of residence, and the man's military card, must be presented to the correct officials. (In contrast, only the birth certificates are required for the religious marriage.) For many of the residents of the squatter settlements, obtaining these documents is extremely difficult, often expensive, and may entail trips to the highland villages in which they were born. If both of the prospective spouses are able to obtain the necessary documents in less than two months' time, they are considered fortunate.

The civil marriage is carried out in a simple manner with only a small amount of fanfare. The actual marriage takes place at the municipal court and is presided over by a judge. Often a number of couples are scheduled for the same time and married simultaneously. The men wear suits and the women wear simple but special dresses. Two witnesses sign with each couple. For the people in the squatter settlements these witnesses become *padrino and madrina de matrimonio civil*, a status of negligible to moderate importance in an individual's network of alliances. The ceremony itself is brief and businesslike and is generally followed by a small party at the home of one set of parents. Only the padrinos and members of the familia de la casa are invited for a meal and some toasting. The civil marriage ceremony is carried out primarily for legal expediency and is not an important social event. As with most changes in status, there is the naming of padrinos and toasting with beer. Lacking, however, is the congregation of kinsmen and paisanos, the dancing, and the opulent feasting which marks the more socially important religious marriage.

The Religious Marriage

The form and the date of the religious ceremony depends primarily on the resources at the disposal of both sets of parents. Often the religious wedding is postponed for months or years until sufficient capital and resources have been accumulated and there is some indication that the relationship between the couple is a stable one. The religious wedding is a social extravaganza on a grand scale. The actual church ceremony is viewed as only one small and formal segment of the celebration.

Lucho and María, who were both nineteen, had lived together at the home of her parents for a year and a half. They were paisanos who had known each other for seven years, ever since Lucho's family migrated to Lima and constructed a home in Ciudadela Chalaca in a housing cluster of paisanos from Ancash. Lucho had been a member of the "group" to which María's older brother also belonged. This group of boys, all of whom were paisanos and many of whom were kin, often gathered in the evenings in front of one of the houses. There, standing or sitting on the remnants of a wall destroyed in an earthquake, they joked and talked and watched the life of the streets. At one point they organized a soccer team. A few years later a group of them organized a band which played the modern "Latin rhythms." Since Lucho often frequented María's house because of his association with her older brother and because Lucho and María were paisanos and thus were both present at many of the parties and other paisano functions, they had the opportunity to become acquainted and later began to live together.

Preparations for the wedding — making reservations for the church and the meeting hall where the mass and party were to be held, obtaining and preparing food, and making or buying clothing — had begun weeks in advance. Engraved invitations were sent by the bride's family to 380 households, most of whose members were kin and paisanos. A few costeños who were friends of the young couple were also invited. All those who attended the wedding gave a gift to the couple prior to the wedding date.

The day before the wedding the bride's family slaughtered and dressed the pig that they had been raising for three years. Preparation of the food, the domain of the bride's family, was begun by the bride's mother, her sisters, and four aunts. The bride's dress and the dresses of the two bridesmaids (the bride's first cousins) and the flower girl (her younger sister) had been rented for the occasion. The padrino and madrina, as is customary, had been selected by the mother of the bride. The church, which was located less than a mile from Ciudadela Chalaca, was decorated with flowers. To most of the guests, who enter a church only during weddings, this was just the beginning of the lavish ostentation that followed. The mass began at eight o'clock in the evening with about two hundred people in attendance. It lasted forty-five minutes and included organ music at the appropriate times. A photographer hired by the family of the bride snapped pictures throughout the mass and party. The grandeur of the church made the entire ceremony very impressive to people coming from their small homes in the squatter settlement.

The parents of the couple play a passive role during this segment of the wedding. It is the priest and the church organization that handle the details, and the padrino who escorts the bride to the altar and gives her away. The mass is viewed by the guests as a necessary prelude to the sumptuous all-night party which follows and which allows the parents of the bride and groom direct and highly visible expression of their control of resources. The party is also, for those in attendance, an opportunity to enjoy themselves dancing, eating, and drinking and to exhibit their solidarity to their paisano group. The entire wedding ceremony — the mass and the party — functions as a node in reciprocity in which a major shift of obligations occurs between kin members who put on the party and those who attend. Reciprocity is the glue which cements social relationships, and the wedding mass and party is the most spectacular opportunity for those living in the squatter settlement to publicly verify and expand their network of relationships.

Most of the women in attendance were dressed in their best clothes, bright cotton or velvet dresses of urban design which they save for just such an occasion and a contrast to the somber, often patched and ragged clothing they wear every day in the squatter settlement. Some of the older women were dressed in highland styles of dark full skirts and bright sweaters. Many women also had teased and lacquered hairstyles, while other women wore their everyday pony-tails or braids. The men were dressed in white shirts and dark suits.

Following the short mass the bride and groom and the padrinos were driven to the hall where the party was to be held in a black, late-model car that had been hired by the padrinos. The guests left the church and took public means of transportation to the party. The hall consisted of a rather plain room approximately fifty by one hundred feet. At one end was a small platform for the band. The room was decorated with streamers of crepe paper and was lined by rows of chairs. More than two hundred people eventually filled the room. Behind the band platform was the door to a small room where the food which had been prepared at the bride's house was served and the dishes washed. After most of the guests had arrived at the hall, Lucho's sister passed out rice to be thrown at the newlyweds when they entered. The band, which played Latin rhythms throughout the night, first rather stiffly played a waltz while the bride danced with the padrino and the groom danced with the madrina as the guests watched approvingly. Then the bride and groom, each set of parents, and the padrinos stood in a row in front of the band to receive congratulations from the guests.

Then the dancing began. This was the time the younger friends and kinsmen of the bride and groom had been waiting for. The older men in their dark suits at first stood stiffly around the room, but they soon passed the beer and began the traditional toasting. Champagne was passed around to all of the guests by the mothers of the couples and their closest female kinsmen. Later, hors d'oeuvres consisting of sweet pastries and small meat sandwiches were served from large platters to all of the guests. Toasts of beer by the male relatives of the bride and groom continued throughout the night. Between dances, when the band was taking a break, the men who carried out the toasting replenished the supply of beer. With a flourish they carried in the cases of beer which had been stored in the back room. As the cases became empty, they were ostentatiously stacked to the side of the room. By dawn, none of the guests had failed to note that sixty cases of beer, three large cauldrons of chicha (homemade maize beer), and numerous bottles of *aguardiente* (cane alcohol) had been consumed.

At midnight, to the delight of all present, a second band strode into the hall. This was a group that the groom's uncle had traveled to the highlands to hire; their instruments consisted of one harp, three saxophones, two violins, and one clarinet. They began playing the traditional huaynos and the guests, young and old, began to dance in couples or in large groups with a sense of enjoyment and abandon that had been lacking before. A bean salad was served, followed by *carapulcra*, the traditional pork dish served at weddings. This was the bride's family pig that had been slaughtered the day before. Dancing, toasting, and eating continued until six in the morning when the guests began to leave for home.

The bride and groom returned to María's family's home where they had been living. Both sets of parents also returned home and slept a few hours. At mid-morning, as is customary, Lucho's parents arrived and awakened the household where Lucho and María were living and invited them to their house, where they all continued to dance to recorded huaynos and drink beer until the evening.

In the days following the wedding the participants, the guests, and even those who did not attend began the customary analysis of what had occurred. Much of the rating of the festivities was based on cold critical calculations of the amount of food and liquor distributed and the general expenses involved in various aspects of the celebration. The mother of the bride commented, "It all went off without incident. And they say that if the wedding goes off well, then the marriage will also do well." The groom said, "Yes, at our wedding, there was food for everyone, not like some other weddings I've been to. I went to a wedding the other day in which they provided only six cases of beer and then took up a collection for more. This looked very bad, especially since they were people with money." The women tended to comment on the food, while the men commented on the alcoholic beverages. The remarks from the youthful kin and friends of the bride and groom were primarily positive. They enjoyed the bands and the dancing. On the other hand, comments by the more mature guests were mixed and included criticisms such as, "The dress of the bride looked as though it had been rented at least twice before"; "The priest was not very agreeable; they could have paid more for a better one"; "The champagne tasted like beer to me"; "They gave plates of food just to the kinsmen and friends that they chose"; "The band was so-so"; "I've been to other weddings where the plates were bigger and piled high." An awareness of this critical bent of the guests at all weddings assures continued striving for elaborate festivities.

These critical comments may seem surprising when one recalls the comparative sumptuousness of the wedding and the expenses both families incurred in proportion to their modest incomes. The groom's family's entire source of income is a small fruitstand at the market located in Ciudadela Chalaca. The bride's family has a slightly higher income since the father works in a factory, the mother works part-time in another factory, and the eldest son drives a delivery truck. Each family's income is between 6,000 and 9,000 soles per month. Each set of parents estimated that they spent at least 30,000 soles on the wedding. This figure was corroborated by various other individuals who had astutely figured the costs.

The following list gives an idea of how expenses were divided and shared between the two families.

Bride's family
    Bride's dress and the family's clothing
    Half the cost of church and reception hall
    Food and food service
    Invitations
    Photographers
    Gifts to padrinos

Groom's family
    Two bands
    Liquor
    Half the cost of church and reception hall
    Groom's and the family's clothing

Padrinos
    The rings
    The car to take the bride and groom to the church, the
        reception hall, and home
    Their own clothing

The groom
      The car to take padrinos to the church, to the reception hall,
      and home

All of these items entailed both a certain amount of expense as
well as collaboration among kinsmen. For example, some of the items
of food provided by the bride's family were extremely expensive. In
this case the family had raised its own pig, thus saving the 3,000 to
4,000 soles which a pig would cost. The bride's family also had to
provide the plates and silverware on which to serve the food. Most
of the 75 plates which were used had been borrowed from kinsmen.
Each plate was washed and refilled a number of times in order to
serve all the guests. Likewise, 45 forks were borrowed and 30 were
purchased (20 of the forks were lost during the wedding and had to
be replaced). The bride's family also had to borrow and purchase
enough glasses for the guests to drink both champagne and beer. The
bride's dress cost 1,400 soles to rent, even though, as the mother of the
bride admitted readily, it had been used two times before. Clothing
for the bride's side of the family also included rental of the flower girl's
dress and purchase of new clothing for the entire family. All of the
women of the immediate family of the bride and groom had had their
hair professionally styled, at a cost of 100 to 200 soles each. Payment
for the mass, which cost 1,700 soles and would have been more had
two priests officiated, was divided between the families of the bride
and groom.

The groom's family's largest expense was for the sixty cases of
beer at 150 soles per case, totalling 9,000 soles. The first band charged
4,000 soles; the cost of the band brought from the highlands and paid
for by the groom's uncle was undisclosed but must have been considerable. The estimates of 30,000 soles paid by each family does not
include the large amount of labor needed to prepare the food and so
forth. Four months after the wedding, the bride's mother indicated
that they were still paying off some of their debts.

Religious weddings in the squatter settlements have become more
elaborate but shorter. In the mid-1960s most of the parties were held
in the home of the parents of the bride, but by 1974 rental of a public
hall for the occasion was much preferred by any family which could
possibly manage the expense. Other innovations observed in 1974
included hired waiters who served the food and a three-tiered wedding
cake decorated with concealed flashing lights. Wedding celebrations
in the highlands habitually last for days, while the longest wedding I
observed in the squatter settlements lasted from Saturday until Mon-
day night, and most are over within twenty-four hours.

COMPADRAZGO

Compadrazgo is a formalized alliance which creates fictive ties of kinship. It is a common phenomenon throughout most of Latin America. In the squatter settlements of Lima compadrazgo is a formal relationship which strengthens existing ties (both kin and non-kin) and provides a path by which alliances may be extended beyond an existing network.

Some forms of compadrazgo are taken more seriously and imply a longer-term relationship than others. For example, the padrinos who are chosen as sponsors for the baptism of a child or for a marriage establish a relationship of much more importance than those who are padrinos at a *cortepelo* (first hair-cutting of a child) or at the baptism of a newly constructed house or new television set. Padrinos, therefore, are the sponsors of an individual or object, while the individuals being sponsored are called *ahijados*. The sponsors are *compadres* to the parents of individuals being sponsored. Every individual in the squatter settlement has numerous compadrazgo ties. In some instances, kin or paisanos are chosen as padrinos, thus strengthening existing ties. In other instances, the most common practice is to look for appropriate padrinos from outside the existing network of alliances, thus opening up new options for interaction and perhaps upward mobility.

Like other alliances the compadrazgo relationship is founded on reciprocity, which is the basis for a trust relationship. In a compadrazgo relationship established outside an existing network of alliances, preference is shown for choosing someone of influence and power in a higher social class. For example, a migrant may be fortunate enough to establish compadrazgo ties with a schoolteacher or the manager in a factory, thus providing his family with partial access to middle-class individuals. It is common for a woman who has worked as a domestic in the home of a well-to-do couple to ask them to act as madrina and padrino for one of her children, thus establishing a formal tie of reciprocity. This form of alliance is another means by which adaptation to the city is effected. From the point of view of the person of higher class, compadrazgo ties with individuals living in the squatter settlements may prove valuable in terms of prestige and of assistance in various tasks requiring the skills and willingness which the migrants possess.

Among those living in the squatter settlements compadrazgo is also commonly used as a means of coping with the dilemma of allegiance to the family of orientation and the family of procreation. In extended families in which siblings have married men or women who may be paisanos but not kin, it is common for a compadre bond to be established between two con-cuñados to heighten trust and the ability to work cooperatively. For example, three brothers living in Dulanto are each married to women who are primas hermanas to one another. These marriages fit the preferential pattern discussed earlier. However, the fourth brother married a woman who was a paisana and yet no kinsman of her husband's sibling's spouses. Thus, when this fourth sibling's first child was born, the couple asked the eldest sibling and his wife to act as padrino and madrina at the infant's baptism, one function of which was to draw the mother of the infant into a compadre/comadre relationship with her affines. Faron (1960:451) notes a similar situation in a coastal Peruvian community: "The *Compadrazgo* relationship is sometimes contracted between brothers and often between cousins or other close relatives. . . . *Compadrazgo* between relatives tends to do two things: 1) reinforce solidarity between persons and their families and 2) extend the incest barrier to those persons immediately involved." The more powerful and influential individuals in the squatter settlements are generally asked to become padrinos more often than the less powerful. Power and influence depend not only on wealth and social class, but also on factors such as birth order. For instance, in the example just cited in which the con-cuñado relationship was strengthened through the establishment of a compadrazgo tie, it was with the eldest sibling that this bond was created. In the squatter settlements the eldest siblings tend to have numerous compadrazgo relationships. It is not uncommon for an eldest sibling to have forty or fifty compadres; having numerous compadres perpetuates power and influence. The eldest sibling is often asked to be a padrino as the representative of the sibling group, thus expanding his or her individual alliances as well as the alliances of the sibling unit.

ECONOMIC ALLIANCES

Nonformalized alliances for economic ends are formed between vendors and their clients at many levels of interaction in the squatter settlements. The alliances are based on past transactions in which cash is exchanged for goods. This form of reciprocity becomes an informal alliance only when repetition establishes a degree of trust, trust to provide quality service and trust in ready payment. The economic alliance, because it is nonformalized, is nonbinding after each transaction. Most of the economic alliances in the squatter settlements are established between vendors and buyers in the marketplaces and housefront stores in Ciudadela Chalaca and Dulanto. Although a number of women in the market sell potatoes side by side, each has her "clients," that is, shoppers who always buy from her because she has the kind of produce they like, gives them a discount, or is a paisana. In turn, the vendors who sell goods at the local markets of Ciudadela Chalaca and Dulanto have similar client-vendor relationships with the wholesalers at the central market where they purchase their goods. Again, the choice of establishing a vendor-client relationship at the central market is influenced by not only the quality of products sold and discounts, but also whether vendors and clients are paisanos. Even individuals living in the squatter settlements who sell prepared foods or offer services in their home develop a circle of clients. The vendor-client relationship demonstrates that even such mundane activities as small daily purchases at the marketplace are marked by personal interaction based on a shared understanding of reciprocity and the need for an ongoing trust relationship.

THE DULANTO BLOCK ASSOCIATION

In the squatter settlements voluntary associations which demonstrate any viability are based on preexisting alliance networks. Members are recruited through extension of kin ties as in marriage or by such means as compadrazgo. For example, one of the largest cooperatives in Ciudadela Chalaca has continued to function for twelve years because the members are simultaneously tied to one another in kin and paisano networks which are overlaid by marriage and compadrazgo alliances. The concept of corporate membership is not a natural one to the residents of the squatter settlements, who instead visualize social interaction in terms of a network of alliances.

A block association established in Dulanto represents a clear contrast in many respects to the traditional reciprocal exchange among kin and paisanos that is so common in Ciudadela Chalaca. In August 1973 a group of neighbors living in one of the blocks in Dulanto decided to develop an association that would provide an organizational base for reciprocal aid in house construction. By this date all of the households on their block had been in Dulanto for almost six months. Few had progressed further than starting to dig the trenches for their house foundations. There were no kinship affiliations among the twenty-two

In clear contrast to the traditional reciprocal exchange among kin and paisanos, neighbors in Dulanto organized themselves into block associations to aid one another in house construction. The group here pours the cement for a lower foundation.

families on the block; few were paisanos, and only three had previously lived in Ciudadela Chalaca and knew one another slightly for that reason. One individual was particularly enthusiastic about the possibility of a block association, for he was familiar with similar associations established in the area. He spoke to various neighbors, and when they in turn conferred as a group with government representatives who offered technical advice and limited use of equipment, the association was formally established.

Much of the enthusiasm and optimism initially exhibited was the result of not only the prospect of rapid house construction but also the pervasive belief found in much of Peru that individuals from the Andean highlands have a great deal of skill, almost an innate ability, to cooperate in communal projects (see Patch 1959). Because of the need to interact with individuals who were of only short acquaintance, were neither kin nor paisanos, and with whom trust had not been built up through years of reciprocal interaction, however, the collaboration was not as smooth as expected.

The association initially had twenty-one member households and an elected president, secretary, and treasurer. It was determined that materials such as bricks, bags of cement, and steel reinforcing rods could be purchased by the association in wholesale quantities, providing savings that would not have been possible with individual household purchases. Wheelbarrows, shovels, hammers, and other tools could be pooled for block use, thus avoiding the need for each household to purchase them. Sand to mix with the cement and gravel to add to the foundations could be brought from the river, two blocks distant, through communal effort. The construction to be carried out according to the official blueprints was to take place every Sunday and on holidays on a rotating basis among the houses, ideally creating a form of balanced reciprocity similar to that which characterizes many kin and paisano relationships. It was decided that each member of the association would also put 200 soles per week into a fund with which building materials would be purchased as they were needed. Those who did not contribute their labor would be fined 100 soles per workday missed. As one member pointed out, the ideal system would save the members money through wholesale purchase of materials and group labor.

During the fall of 1973 members of the association met twice a month in the evenings at midweek to discuss their plans. A government representative attended two of these meetings to offer his approval and his services as a consultant, should the need arise. Work on Sundays consisted primarily of the communal gathering of sand and rocks from the river. Not all members were able to furnish the required 200 soles per week, yet many did. Fifty sacks of cement were purchased and stored at the home of one of the members; three of the sacks were ruined when the roof leaked during an unusually wet period. The first three and a half months of the association's existence were characterized by enthusiasm and optimism. Although most interaction among neighbors was still marked by the reserve which is often shown for non-kin, many neighbors began to interact with some frequency.

Late one night in December, however, the president and the treasurer of the association disappeared with the funds that the members had been saving since August. The two lots vacated by their families were assigned to new families. At this point, the association was left with no funds and a feeling of mistrust among the members. All of its functions ceased. One month later three past members began to discuss reorganizing the association. Sixteen of the former members joined, and by March 1974 meetings and work on Sundays had begun.

At this stage most of the lots had trenches for the foundations, and the Sunday work from March until July consisted primarily of filling the trenches with cement and placing the steel reinforcing rods. Some weeks, work went ahead rapidly. On other Sundays few members showed up or there were accusations that certain members always took the easier jobs or that some worked too slowly and rested too often. The only official excuse for avoiding the 100 soles fine for not appearing to work on Sundays was illness. A complaint often heard was that an individual was counting his hangover as an illness. The association did not have as much sanctioning power as an extended kin network to compel members to appear for work.

The association's regulations maintained that the household for which the Sunday work was carried out was to provide all who worked with a substantial midday meal. Many women commented that the expense of the meal was almost equivalent to the cost of hiring the same number of workers. There were also complaints about the unevenness in quality of the meals served, and an unresolved problem existed as to whether the household where the work was carried out should also provide beer. By July, when the lower foundations had been completed, there remained only eleven members. At this time, approximately one year after the initial founding of the association, work could begin on the upper foundations. By the end of September, one more family had dropped out, but upper foundations had been completed for the remaining ten members. The funds were then depleted by a wholesale purchase of bricks, and the remaining members decided to call a halt to the weekly construction, deciding that the brickwork could be carried out individually. The association's primary function had been completed with the pouring of the foundations. Although the association was not formally disbanded, it became inactive. A number of the members expressed a sense of relief. Cooperation had not been as effortless as they had expected. An overall assessment of the activities of the association was made by one member when he said, "In the end we made some progress in our construction, yet it seems that we had too many problems. And if we really managed to save money, I just don't know. I think that it might have worked out better if I had just worked with my relatives even though there are not too many here."

In contrast to the pattern of alliance formation in Ciudadela Chalaca, the block association within Dulanto not only was faced with the problems of establishing interaction based on trust in the absence of kin ties among the association members but was dealing with a limited and defined group of participants in which no options for expanding membership were available. In the block association the members had the common goal of constructing their houses with minimal expense, but the lack of a previously existing network of kin or alliance ties was a hindrance to the development of trust and the smooth attainment of the shared goal. In contrast, in Ciudadela Chalaca, through the mutual-aid network and with the expectation of reciprocity, the labor force necessary for house construction was mobilized and the task carried out. From the viewpoint of the migrants, the use of personal networks is the most expedient manner of insuring trust and reciprocity in relationships and in creating the flexibility necessary to face the dynamically shifting options that may occur during the process of adaptation.

RITES OF INTENSIFICATION

CHAPTER 9

A basic component of any sort of celebration in the squatter settlements is the gathering of people together: to feel the satisfaction and security of belonging to a group and to renew the relationship of trust and reciprocity which ideally characterizes relationships. One of the advantages of living in the city which is often mentioned by the migrants is the ease and frequency with which people are able to get together in comparison to the relatively isolated highland existence. A positive stress is given to being with other people, and the frequent celebrations provide an opportunity to interact with large groups of people in an often intense manner. The second common characteristic of any celebration or rite is the display and consumption of food and alcoholic beverages. As discussed previously, food and drink are important symbolic expressions of hospitality and trust and serve as essential resources in reciprocity. At many celebrations music and dancing lasts all night or even a number of days and nights. Usually there is also the choosing of padrinos.

Each individual has an extensive personal network among kin, paisanos, and non-kin which allows admittance into a wide array of celebrations. Thus, each individual has the potential to participate in many events if he or she so chooses. Added to the frequently occurring rites of passage are those events which depend on the yearly cycle. These include celebrations of the home village patron saint's day, the carnival celebrations including the *Yunsa*, or tree-cutting, and the national holidays. Many informal get-togethers occur during the weekends to celebrate such diverse and individual events as the welcome home of a kinsman who has been in the highlands, a farewell party for one who is about to leave for a highland visit, or a dinner to celebrate a young person's graduation from high school. Often so many events occur simultaneously that an individual has to choose which to attend.

RITES OF PASSAGE

In the squatter settlements a number of terms applied to different age categories also correspond loosely to the developmental cycle of the individual and the nuclear family. They are *bebé, niño, joven, recién casados, joven matrimonios, familias maduras,* and *los ancianos.*

Bebé is a term used for an infant, male or female, although in a more formal situation the sex of an infant may be distinguished by the terms *hombre* (man) (or *hombrecito*) or *mujer* (woman) (or *mujercita*). The infant remains a bebé until he is able to eat adult foods and walk, usually between one and a half and two years of age. At this time, dependency on the mother is lessened and the child begins to develop a deep bond with his siblings. Until sometime after puberty children are referred to as *niños* (boys) or *niñas* (girls). Except for the fact of their sheer numbers, their influence in the decision-making processes in most nuclear families is minimal, as is their prestige.

The celebration of a girl's fifteenth birthday may be carried out in the urban manner with a fiesta which marks the entrance into young adulthood. Occasionally boys may be given a party at their eighteenth birthday. However, most boys slip into young adulthood and become jovenes at no specially marked time. One is a joven until a separate household and family of procreation is begun. Until this time the joven continues to live in the house of his or her parents and continues to function as a part of that household unit.

The status of joven is one laden with contradictions, many of them due to the changes resulting from the urbanization process. In the highlands the status of the unmarried young adult is traditionally one with little prestige and power. As Fuenzalido (1970:79) points out,

the low prestige of the jovenes in the highlands and the lack of opportunity for achieving economic independence are strong factors that
contribute to the migration of young people to the cities. The age
category of jovenes is not accorded particular prestige in the squatter
settlement, yet because they comprise the group with the most education and with the greatest potential for substantial earnings in the
near future, jovenes are accorded some recognition if not outright
respect. The jovenes of the squatter settlements by and large consider
themselves Limeños or Chalacos and have had little firsthand experience with the highlands and the traditional way of life found there.
The concept of *mi tierra* (my homeland) so often nostalgically referred
to by their parents has been replaced by the concept of *mi barrio*
(my neighborhood), where they have spent their lives. Because of their
lifelong exposure to the urban setting and their access to educational
facilities, it is the jovenes who feel at home in the city and who have
mastered some of the skills of urban living. Although the joven in the
squatter settlement has more prestige vis-à-vis his relatives of similar
age in the highlands, he still must face a world in which he is most
often considered of only marginal consequence. For example, at the
community level in the squatter settlement the jovenes are never
directly involved in political activities. Unmarried youths always continue to live in the home and under the dominance of their parents
or another close kinsperson. Many jovenes who have obtained a secondary school education still have problems finding employment, and
when they do find jobs, their pay is very low.

With the gradual consolidation of a conjugal union and with the
coming of children, a couple begins to acquire a new status, that of
adults, recién casados or joven matrimonios. The early years of marriage and of raising small children are considered a time of hardship.
It is a time when plans are made and savings are begun. As the years
go by, the nuclear family of procreation ideally begins to consolidate
economic gains and becomes a familia madura, or mature family. A
peak period of economic wealth and social prestige is reached some-
where between the ages of 35 and 50, at which time the eldest children
are almost at the age of forming their own families of procreation. It
is in this period that men and women are the most active and influential
in community-wide activities. This is the time that one's personal network reaches the maximum extension, and an individual is most often
chosen as sponsor for an expensive yet prestige-generating saint's day
fiesta or may decide that the time is right to arrange for an elaborate
wedding, quinceañera celebration for a child, or baptism of a grandchild. During this period in life one may also offer hospitality to

long-term visiting kinsmen. Thus, it is during middle age that one fulfills the most extensive responsibilities toward kin and paisanos and
at the same time gains the most prestige.

After the age of about 50, there is a rather rapid decline into old
age and one becomes an anciano with the accompanying inability to
earn sufficient capital to control resources. Power and prestige decrease
and the network of influence shrinks. Within the squatter settlements
few of the original migrants have reached this stage, but this decline
of power and prestige is the general picture which is painted regarding
old age.

Baptisms and Cortepelo

Most parents who live in the squatter settlements would like to
have their children baptized. In reality fewer than one half of them
manage to baptize their children. Baptism in Ciudadela Chalaca or
Dulanto includes the relatively short and inconspicuous church ceremony as well as the elaborate and often expensive meal and all-night
party which follows. A baptism such as this is a major and expensive
undertaking in terms of organization, effort, and money. Ideally, a
child should be baptized before the age of two, but often a family
waiting for the right financial or personal circumstances or the right
padrino or madrina to offer to share the expenses may delay until the
child is four or five.

Ideally, the cortepelo occurs as a separate rite denoting the attainment of childhood by boys at about two years of age. Both a madrina
and padrino are chosen to cut the first locks of hair and contribute a
gift of cash to the child. In the highlands gifts of land or stock were
common. In the squatter settlements an all-night party follows the
ceremony. A little boy whose hair has not yet been cut often wears a
ponytail at the top of his head until the cortepelo occurs. By 1974 very
few families actually carried through with the cortepelo even though
many mentioned it. As one mother said, "It is too expensive now in the
city." If carried out at all, the cortepelo is usually combined with the
baptism ceremony as one of the first acts of the padrinos after returning
from the baptism in the church.

Birthday Celebrations

The birthday party is an important event for both children and
adults. The term santo (saint or saint's day) is used, although the day
which is celebrated is the anniversary of one's birth and not the saint's

day which an individual's name denotes. The birthday celebration is a time when the entire *familia de la casa* attends a meal and gives appropriate toasts at the home of the person whose birthday it is. Among the adults living in both Ciudadela Chalaca and Dulanto the birthday celebration may be an intimate one with only siblings and their spouses attending, or it may be larger and include other more distant *familia* and *parientes*. The *padrinos* of baptism or of marriage, if they live nearby, are also generally invited to the birthday celebration. The celebration centers on a festive meal.

A child's birthday celebration, while ostensibly commemorating a child's day of birth, is primarily a party for the attending adults. Usually the children are given some punch or another type of sweet and then sent out to play, while the adults eat a large meal and continue to drink far into the night.

Of particular importance is the celebration of the fifteenth birthday of girls. The *quinceañera*, as this birthday is called, is commonly celebrated throughout much of Latin America among the non-Indian populations. Although in highland Peru it is of almost no significance, this ceremony is one urban coastal tradition which many of the migrant families have taken on with a gusto. The fiesta combines many features of both a birthday party and a coming-out party for the girls, who at this age enters young womanhood. Many families whose oldest children were reaching their mid-teens by 1974 chose to make the celebration of the quinceañera an opportunity to demonstrate the degree to which they have prospered since arriving in the city about ten years before. The celebration of the quinceañera is one of the very few instances in which the focus is placed on the *jovenes* rather than the adults who attend. The popularity of the quinceañera party is one indication of the higher status of the *jovenes* in the squatter settlements compared to their age-mates in the highlands.

Weddings

Marriage is of prime importance within the life cycle of any individual and is discussed in detail in Chapter 8.

Wakes and Funerals

Wakes and funerals differ somewhat from other rites of passage in that they often must be carried out with very little forewarning, and thus there is no time to save money and plan in advance. The actual events and their sequence during the mourning period vary not only in response to the economic means of the family and the age of the deceased but also in regard to the highland origin of those involved. Because of the relatively young population in the squatter settlements and the high rate of infant mortality, many of the deaths are those of infants and small children. Adult deaths occur most frequently as the result of accidents or infectious diseases.

After the death the family rents a *capilla ardiente* (four candelabras, a white drape for the wall, and a crucifix) to be set up around the white coffin in which the body is displayed at the wake. The clothing of the deceased may also be placed in the room. The capilla ardiente used for an infant or child is generally simple in contrast to the more elaborate one used for an adult. The expense incurred by the family of the deceased at the wake and burial is often a reflection of its economic standing within the squatter settlement.

During the first day after the death the door of the home is left open so that kinsmen, paisanos, and neighbors may briefly enter and pay their respects to the familia de la casa of the deceased. The wake, or *velorio*, begins on the night of the first day, as friends and relatives continue to stop by to pay their respects and view the body. The following night the wake continues, as kinsmen and paisanos join the immediate family in an all-night vigil. Each guest brings a gift of cognac, coffee, or coca, which is then consumed by those present. The family of the deceased serves a meal at midnight and again in the early morning. The wake of a child may be attended by only a dozen or so kinsmen and the child's padrinos of baptism. However, the wake of a prestigious adult may be attended by hundreds and hundreds of kinsmen, paisanos, and others with whom he or she had been affiliated. The tone of the wake of a child tends to be much lighter than that of the wake of an adult, and peaks of hilarity are often reached. At the wakes of both children and adults, the guests and immediate family members converse and often joke. Those in attendance who are outside the familia de la casa feel it is their duty to "accompany" the close kin of the deceased so that they will not feel lonely nor sad. Burial may occur the afternoon following the wake or may be delayed for another day.

For the funeral of a child the padrinos of baptism carry the coffin in the cemetery or pay for a portion of the funeral expenses. The family of the deceased is expected to provide transportation for the ride to the cemetery. When hundreds of persons desire to attend the burial of an adult, one or two of the buses that run the route between the squatter settlements between Ciudadela Chalaca and Dulanto may be commissioned. Since almost all of the bus drivers who work the routes between Ciudadela Chalaca and Dulanto live in these settlements themselves and may have kin or paisano links to the deceased, the activation

This crowd attending a burial is considered by
some residents to be only a small gathering.

of a reciprocal obligation may be all that is necessary on the part of
the family of the deceased in order to have the service of a bus.

Burial may take place either in the mausoleum at the public
cemetery in Callao or at the "Cementerio de la Regla," an unofficial,
clandestine cemetery that has expanded at a rate only equaled by the
rate of growth of the squatter settlements themselves. Most of those
who choose the public cemetery pay for a temporary niche, tending to
overlook the fact that after three months the bodies are removed and
cremated. It is the rare family which is able to afford a perpetual niche.
On the other hand, the clandestine cemetery offers free burial that is
carried out by the family, which digs the grave and places the coffin.
Its disadvantage lies in the frequency of the graves being disturbed by
the elements, grave robbers, or goats that are pastured nearby. For

those who choose to inter at the public cemetery, a short prayer is offered by a priest who is in attendance. Immediately following the burial, which is carried out rapidly and sometimes accompanied by wails from the women of the immediate family, cognac or rum is served to all present "to purify." Upon leaving the cemetery, all return to the home of the deceased, where they are served another meal and may continue to drink and visit through most of the night. Among some living in the squatter settlements the disposal of the clothing of the deceased is of no issue. However, for others, particularly those who have migrated from the more traditional highland towns, the clothing of the deceased as well as the mourners themselves are ritually washed on the third day after the wake at a small freshwater spring located about a mile and a half from Ciudadela Chalaca. The night following the washing of the clothes a final wake, the "farewell," is carried out and attended primarily by the familia of the deceased.

THE YEARLY CYCLE

The following annual holidays are those which are observed in some way by the residents of Ciudadela Chalaca and Dulanto:

January 1	*Año nuevo* (New Year's Day)
January 6	*Bajada de los Reyes* (Epiphany)
First Saturday of February	Beginning of *Carnaval* (includes *Yunsa* or *Cortamonte*)
Variable date	*Semana Santa* (Easter week)
May 1	*Día del Obrero* (Worker's Day)
May 12	*Día de la Madre* (Mother's Day)
July 26–28	*Fiestas Patrias* (Independence Days)
August 19	*Día de Callao* (Callao Day)
September 22	*Día de primavera* (first day of spring)
October 9	*Día de dignidad nacional* (National Dignity Day)
October 12	*Día de la Raza* (Heritage Day)
October 16–23	*Feria de Octubre* (Observing the Patron Saint day of *Señor de los Milagros*)
November 1	*Todos Santos* (All Saints' Day)
December 9	*Batalla de Ayacucho* (Battle of Ayacucho celebrating independence)
December 25	*Navidad* (Christmas)
December 25–January 1	Festive week

Of particular interest is the shift in the squatter settlements from an emphasis on the agricultural cycle, as was the case in the highlands, to an emphasis on national and religious holidays. For example, the fiestas patrias serve an important function within the squatter settlements by providing a sense of participation in national affairs on the part of those migrants who have come from relatively isolated and nationally uninvolved communities in the highlands.

On many of these public holidays school is not in session and factories and governmental offices are closed. Frequently siblings or other kin informally get together to drink beer, talk, and play zappos. The entire household may go to exhibits of highland dances or a circus; soccer and volleyball tournaments often take place. By 1973 many of the families living in Dulanto were using holidays and long weekends for the construction of their homes.

The Yunsa, or cortamonte, occurs on four Sundays of Lent throughout the squatter settlements. In Ciudadela Chalaca prior to the remodeling the Yunsa was held within a residential clustering of families which had come from Ancash and Huanuco, and the celebration was similar to the version found in their highland communities. In Dulanto and in Ciudadela Chalaca since the remodeling, a more heterogeneous group has participated in the celebration. Three couples act as the padrinos of the event, one supplying drinks, one a band or record player, and one an evergreen tree. The tree is cut and brought to the squatter settlement and "planted" in a deeply dug hole. It is then decorated with paper chains, fruits, and small toys such as squirt guns. In the afternoon beer is served and all of those present dance to highland music. This holiday is also a time for water fights, dousing friends with talc, and other jokes. At a signal from the padrino who has prepared the tree, a couple is handed an axe and given one chance to chop down the tree. The couples that will carry the cargos (duties) of the music and beer the following year are chosen to cut limbs off the tree. The couple that actually cuts down the tree will carry the cargo of supplying and decorating the tree the following year. Dancing and beer-drinking continues past midnight. The majority of those in attendance are kin and paisanos of those holding the cargos. However, particularly in Dulanto, numerous neighbors who have some acquaintance with the padrinos attend and dance actively. The Yunsa is a small celebration, and the cargos which are carried by the three principal couples who act as padrinos are relatively minor. However, the event serves to intensify the interaction within a paisano or residential grouping as well as to provide entertainment. Additionally, the three cargo holders enhance their positions within the community.

THE PATRON SAINT'S FIESTA

An extensive celebration is carried out for the patron saint of the highland village from which a group of paisanos living in Ciudadela Chalaca or Dulanto has migrated. Some paisano groups and individuals in the squatter settlements pay little attention to the saint's fiesta of their home village; some return to their home village to participate in the fiesta, while others carry out their own saint's day celebration in the squatter settlement. Fiestas such as the celebration of the Día de San Pedro, the patron saint of Corongo in Ancash, function to intensify paisano group interaction and define social position.

In 1963, when the fiesta honoring San Pedro was first carried out by the migrants from Corongo, most of the participants lived in a paisano cluster and the main events of the fiesta took place there. The 1974 celebration took place in Ciudadela Chalaca and centered on the two-block area to which most of the former Corongo paisano cluster had been relocated. Some of the former residents of the paisano cluster who had relocated in Dulanto also actively participated in the fiesta.

Día de San Pedro is June 28, but preparation for the fiesta begins well ahead of time, to the extent that some families raise sheep, pigs, and guinea pigs for months or even years in advance to be slaughtered for San Pedro. In fact, in the eyes of the participants, the celebration in honor of San Pedro is a never-ending cycle from one year to the next in which there is a yearly shift from domestic unit to domestic unit which carries the responsibility, or cargo, for sponsoring the festivities. The focus for much of the festivities is a wooden figure of San Pedro a meter and a half tall which was purchased in 1963 by the group of Coronginos who first celebrated this fiesta. The figure of San Pedro is dressed in clothing purchased or sewn and cared for by four women, the *mayorales*. Other pieces of San Pedro's clothing are given to him as part of religious promises. Prior to the remodeling San Pedro was housed during the year in a small cement chapel. After the remodeling San Pedro was kept in the home of the family holding the fiesta cargo until his new chapel was built in October of 1974.

Each year following the fiesta the next *mayordomo*, in this case called the *Juez de Agua*, is chosen to carry the cargo sponsorship the following year. The decision as to who will be Juez de Agua depends both on public consensus and on a person feeling that the time is right to volunteer to serve in this cargo. Although the cargo is technically carried by one person, ultimately it is the entire familia, especially the sibling group, that is responsible for the success or failure of the fiesta. In 1974 the Juez de Agua was Faustino.

The fiesta of San Pedro celebrated in Ciudadela Chalaca is a scaled-down version of the fiesta for San Pedro as celebrated in the highland community of Corongo. For example, in Ciudadela Chalaca in 1974 there were six *pallas*, costumed female dancers, while it was rumored that in Corongo the previous year there had been almost thirty pallas. Two of the major events of the highlands celebration, the running of the bull and the lavish fireworks, are impossible to carry out in the squatter settlement. Nevertheless, the basic form of the celebration which takes place in the squatter settlement follows that which occurs in the highlands, with a focus on processions, feasting, drinking, and dancing.

Beginning on May 11 the figure of San Pedro is housed for a few days at a time in the homes of various fiesta participants, who keep candles lit at his feet in fulfillment of promises they made to him. Besides the social prestige which is obtained through hosting San Pedro, his presence is thought to assure a religious sanctity to the home. Juana recounted that San Pedro was in her home during a time of unusually wet weather in which many of the houses in Ciudadela Chalaca and Dulanto leaked. Juana's entire house was wet, even the family beds. However, the corner in which San Pedro stood remained dry. Juana half-jokingly asked San Pedro, "Why are you punishing me in this way?" The next day she again mentioned the incident and added, "I usually don't joke with San Pedro like that. Usually I speak seriously to him."

During the weeks of *velando*, or lighting candles for San Pedro, the saint is moved from house to house by the *muñador* whose cargo it is to carry the figure during both the velando and the fiesta. On June 25 San Pedro is returned to the home of the Juez de Agua in preparation for the celebration. During the few weeks immediately prior to the celebration, the primary celebrants are occupied with obtaining and preparing food and alcoholic beverages, sewing or renting costumes, hiring a band, and handling the innumerable other details, such as obtaining a municipal permit for the religious procession. All of these duties are delegated to members of a large network of kin and paisanos who are bound in reciprocal relationships to the Juez de Agua.

During the fiesta itself, numerous events occur simultaneously, yet the focus of intensity is in the vicinity of the figure of San Pedro. By nine o'clock on the Friday night on which the fiesta was to begin, a dance enclosure measuring approximately thirty by thirty feet had been set up in the street in front of the house of the Juez de Agua. Food preparation, which had begun days ago in the kitchen of this house, was reaching a crescendo. Paper streamers had been strung along the street. Curious neighbors began to stand expectantly in the vicinity. At eleven o'clock an eleven-member band brought from the highlands for the occasion emerged from a nearby house which was used as a staging area throughout the festivities. In typically eclectic highland form the band included two drums, one cymbal, one violin, three saxophones, two clarinets, and two trombones. The music which the band played throughout the celebrations was typical of Ancash and particularly of the area around Corongo. Likewise, the dancing which occurred throughout the days of the fiesta was the stately rhythmic walking step or the more animated skipping step typical of Corongo, in contrast to the more rousing style of the central highlands. After the band entered the dance enclosure, the Juez de Agua and his wife proudly danced the first dance as hundreds of paisanos and neighbors came to the area. After a few more dances were played, a case of beer was brought out and distributed by the Juez de Agua to the band members. For the remaining three days of the fiesta, the band continued to play, stopping only to drink, eat, and rest occasionally. The figure of San Pedro was brought from the house to a small enclosure outside. At midnight four pre-teen boys (los farolitos or lantern-bearers) danced from the staging area to San Pedro. Each boy carried a paper lantern on a four-foot pole. They were accompanied by two men who played two large drums, one a chiroco and one a roncadora distinguished from a chiroco by a tightly strung cord along one side which produced a vibrating sound accompanying each beat. Each drummer simultaneously played a whistle, creating an eerie effect. The dancing band and the celebrants grew silent and watched without moving as the farolitos and drummers appeared out of the darkness of night, danced briefly in front of San Pedro, and then retreated down the street. The roncadora and chiroco appeared frequently at key points during the next three days.

The band continued to play and dancers flowed out into the surrounding streets. At one in the morning the band left the enclosure and walked to the house that was the staging area. Here they played while the dancing continued in the street. Bottled beer was augmented with large pails of chicha which was served to all participants. The band continued to play as they returned to the enclosed area, and general dancing and ritualized toasting and drinking resumed. Throughout the three-day celebration, candles were placed at the feet of San Pedro by those who had made promises. Around one-thirty in the morning the band was invited into the house of the Juez de Agua, where they were provided with a traditional meal of soup, corn, meat, and potatoes.

At two-thirty the sound of the chiroco and roncadora was again

In procession with San Pedro are two pallas, or costumed women dancers, followed by celebrants playing traditional drums and whistles.

heard from the west, and there appeared a *diablo* (devil) with a two-
faced, horned mask. He wore a long overcoat and carried a whip with
which he struck out at the spectators who came too near. Following
the diablo were twenty dancing *panatawas,* small boys carrying small
whips and dressed in shirts and pants decorated with colored crepe
paper. Beside the panatawas walked their coordinator, an elderly man
who had taught them their dance steps and who was active behind the
scenes in many aspects of the fiesta. Following the panatawas walked
two *angelitos,* or San Miguels, young boys wearing blue dresses over
their pants and horsehair wigs and gold paper crowns. One carried
a paper sword and the other a shield.

Following the angelitos came the lavishly dressed, magnificent pallas, the costumed women dancers. Their ornate costumes consisted of a number of layers of skirts, or *polleras*, and blouses with flowing sleeves which extended more than a foot beyond their fingertips. On their heads were elaborate and heavy headdresses. Their costumes were encrusted with mirrors and artificial jewels, creating a spectacular impression. Their dance, consisting of traditional movements, was sedate and stately. The entire procession entered the dance enclosure and, when joined by the Juez de Agua, began to dance to both the drums and the band. Soon more and more spectators joined in the dancing. Beer continued to be served to the principal celebrants, and the sense of festive enjoyment became intense. Then the entire assemblage left the enclosure and began dancing along the streets of Ciudadela Chalaca. Soon hundreds of people of all ages joined in. The hours of dancing, music, sleeplessness, beer-drinking, and exposure to religiously significant symbols had created their effect, and there developed a general feeling of group euphoria. Ritual drinking and dancing continued until six in the morning. Then there followed a general slackening of festivities as many people went home for a few hours of sleep. Dancing continued only in the house of the Juez de Agua and in two of his siblings' homes nearby. The figure of San Pedro had been taken inside until midday.

At eleven in the morning the men who played the chiroco and roncadora emerged from the home of one of the siblings of the Juez de Agua where they had been resting. As they played and walked along the streets, the panatawas emerged and fell into line, dancing behind the drummers. Soon they were joined by the band, the pallas, the angelitos, the diablo, and a throng of spectators. They slowly circled the block, gathering a crowd as they went. Meanwhile, the figure of San Pedro was carried out of the home of the Juez de Agua and tied securely to the *anda,* the platform on which he was carried in procession to the church seven blocks distant. Although this is the church closest to Ciudadela Chalaca, with almost no exception those who live there enter it only during community events such as the fiesta of San Pedro. Large wreaths of roses and chrysanthemums were affixed to the platform. The figure and the platform were so heavy that at least four persons were needed to carry them at any one time, and many people took turns. The procession to and from the church was the only time that the figure of San Pedro was carried in procession, and it was also the most solemn portion of the festivities. Yet the pallas and panatawas continued to dance to the music provided by the two large drums and the band. The church nearest Ciudadela Chalaca is located in the midst of a government-constructed apartment complex, through which the procession of approximately three hundred people slowly made its way. The mass, which had been prearranged, was short and was preceded by the priest's comment that "now that you have had your party, it is time for the religious part." This statement was later repeatedly criticized by the Coronginos, who said that the priest never realizes that every cargo in the fiesta is carried out as a religious act for San Pedro. On leaving the church, the procession slowly returned to Ciudadela Chalaca.

All the adults who had carried a cargo associated with the fiesta and numerous other kin, paisanos, and compadres of the Juez de Agua and his siblings were then invited to a lavish midday meal. No criollos were invited. Here the line was drawn between the criollo neighbors who had watched the festivities and perhaps danced and the Coronginos or those closely allied with Coronginos. Because of the large number of people involved and the limited seating space, the meal was served in four shifts and took more than two hours to complete. The Juez de Agua directed the meal while his wife and near female kin who had prepared the food served it. Large trays of *mote* (hominy) were served, followed by soup, then a rice-and-lamb dish, and finally guinea pigs and potatoes in a hot sauce. In the traditional manner of indicating the generosity of the Juez de Agua, all of the servings were of tremendous size and more than anyone was able to eat. Ritual toasts of beer and chicha were made throughout the meal, and gaiety and ribald jokes were the rule.

Following the meal, the band, the Juez de Agua, and the pallas returned to the dancing enclosure and continued to dance and drink beer. About one hundred and fifty paisanos and neighbors joined them. Around five in the afternoon the band and all of the participants began again to dance through the streets of Ciudadela Chalaca, finally ending at the house of the man who would be the Juez de Agua the following year. He was also a primo hermano of the Juez from the present year. The large red flags of San Pedro were presented to the new Juez de Agua and his wife by those who had presided at the present celebration. Drinking and dancing continued in the house and in the street in front of the house of the next year's Juez de Agua. When the band left at seven, beer-drinking and dancing continued to the chiroco and roncadora as well as to recorded music. By early evening many people had stumbled off for a few hours of rest at their homes, but the principal celebrants continued to dance and drink until after midnight. On Saturday evening the dance enclosure was removed and the figure of San Pedro was taken back inside Faustino's house where *velando* was continued. On Sunday morning a few of the celebrants continued to

The Juez de Agua, sponsor of the celebration, dances with
the pallas during the Fiesta of San Pedro in Ciudadela Chalaca.

dance and drink, but the majority were *componiendo el cuerpo* (recu-
perating). The pallas had removed their costumes and were at the marketplace as usual. The other participants were preparing for the events
that were to follow that afternoon.

At about four o'clock in the house of Faustino the ceremony of the
ofrendamiento, or *quitando el mal de cuerpo* (removal of evil, both sins
and illness, from the body), was performed. The large living room of
the house was filled with people. A red cloth was placed on the floor
and on top of that a heavy woolen blanket from the highlands. The
Juez de Agua was led to the blanket by the woman whom he had chosen
as his madrina (a cousin) for the occasion. He lay face down on the
blanket and the muñador rubbed the figure of San Pedro up and down

his body three times, pressing quite hard. Then the madrina helped Faustino up, they embraced, and she placed 10 soles in a plate held by the chief mayoral, who stood in front of San Pedro. In turn the mayoral handed Faustino's madrina a red carnation. The process was repeated with Faustino's wife. While she was being rubbed by San Pedro, her padrino also whipped her with some force with his belt. Outside the door the chiroco and roncadora played as three of the pallas and the Juez de Agua danced. Many of those who had participated in the celebration as well as other neighbors participated in the cleansing act, each choosing a madrina or padrino who then contributed a small amount of money toward the maintenance of San Pedro. During the ceremony chicha was passed out to all present and many joined in the dancing outside.

Following this ceremony San Pedro was prepared to be moved to his new home at the house of the man who would serve as Juez de Agua in the coming year. White clothing was placed on San Pedro and the figure was carried outside and secured on the anda. Accompanied by the music of the chiroco and the roncadora, the dancing pallas, and numerous spectators, the figure of San Pedro was carried to the living room of the next Juez de Agua. Here the figure was secured on a box, and flowers and candles were placed on the floor around him. Drinking and dancing to the music of the chiroco and roncadora as well as to recorded music continued until after midnight, when the last celebrants returned to their homes. The fiesta was over, and the night was very quiet outside.

The expense of such a fiesta is tremendous, estimated by some as more than 30,000 soles, an amount which does not include the labor expended or all of the materials. The greatest burden of expense and responsibility rests on the shoulders of the Juez de Agua and his immediate family. However, many of the duties associated with putting on the fiesta are spread throughout the kin and paisano network controlled by the Juez de Agua (Fig. 9.1).

In addition to the formal cargos there exist numerous unnamed cargos, such as sewing the dresses for the pallas, serving the chicha, constructing the dance enclosure, and hosting of the band members and other visitors. Some of the cargos or the incidental aid during the fiesta were provided by persons who were tied to the Juez de Agua through such forms of alliance as compadrazgo or vendor-client relationships. The fiesta not only holds religious significance and acts as public entertainment but also functions to intensify paisano group solidarity and to enhance the prestige of the Juez de Agua and his immediate kinsmen. The pivotal role of the Juez de Agua was shown by his exaggerated

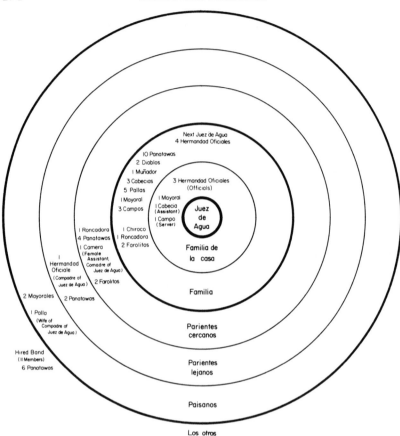

Los otros

Figure 9.1 Principal official participants in the fiesta
of San Pedro and their relationship to the Juez de Agua.

hospitality toward all who attended, his overseeing of the serving
of the meals, his insisting that all of the plates be heaped with food,
and his exuberant commands that more cases of beer be brought out.
As a public event the fiesta of San Pedro is filled with symbolic significance to the paisanos who have migrated from Corongo. The event
stresses paisano collaboration and unity. The fiesta also activates and
stimulates a nexus of reciprocal obligations that continue to be revived
throughout the following year, thereby serving to keep individual
networks functioning as useful aids during urban adaptation.

    In contrast, an alternate solution to participation in the saint's day
fiesta is the common practice of returning to the highland village. Many
of the residents of the squatter settlement who work as wage laborers

arrange their vacation times to coincide with the saint's fiesta of their home village, or if they are self-employed they take this time off to return to the highlands. Although many people may be able to afford to attend the fiesta only on occasion, the years in which they do return are important events in their lives to be remembered and recounted with vivid nostalgia for months or years to come. Within a large paisano cluster, such as that from Apurimac with 84 contiguous households before the relocation, there would generally be at least one paisano at any given time visiting the homeland and returning with news of events and kin who have remained there.

Most migrants find the increased opportunity for social interaction in the squatter settlements to be advantageous to their strategies for urban adaptation and eventual upward mobility. It is during the rites of intensification, as modified to fit the urban situation, that the full complement of kin and paisanos in the city are drawn together to participate in an event that renews and strengthens their unity and ongoing reliance on one another. Both the gregarious social interaction and the large amount of planning and amassing of resources that are necessary to carry out many of the rites of intensification represent much of what for the migrants are the distinct advantages of urban living: a large personal network of potential supporters and the ability to earn enough income to sponsor elaborate displays of wealth. The migrants' sense of community and sense of control over their lives, exemplified in the fiesta of San Pedro, contribute to their positive view of themselves and of their future.

ADAPTATION TO URBAN LIFE

The adaptation of a highland village fiesta to an urban situation is just one example of the migrants' flexibility in adapting the resources at their command to the squatter settlement setting. When a highlander arrives in Lima, for example, he is already part of a network of kin and thus usually is able to move in with a sibling already in the barriada. The strong sibling tie manifested in the squatter settlements is partly an adaptation to the absence of the parental generation: the eldest sibling has become the head of the barriada family. If a sibling is not available, the network of kin is flexible enough that a newly arrived migrant may count on a first cousin, aunt, or uncle for help.

Once established temporarily in a sibling's household, the new resident quickly expands his network of kin and alliances, a process necessary both for his survival and for his eventual development of social prestige and upward mobility. He is already at the center of a kin network but must involve himself in reciprocal obligations if he is to activate the network in his favor. He then forms a network of alliances with in-laws and compadres. The process of alliance formation is another resource brought to the squatter settlements from the highland villages and adapted to the new setting. For example, the migrant may seek as padrinos for his children an employer or a school teacher. Thus the success of the migrants in adapting to urban life depends on their ability to adapt the kin and alliance systems of their highland villages to life in the city. Accomplishing goals of education, housing, obtaining urban amenities and upward mobility, as well as maintaining a sense of well-being and a positive view of self, all depend on the migrants' facility of adaptation. In turn this adaptation is possible because the migrants are able to utilize existing core relationships, to form extensive alliances, to gain a sense of control of their lives and because flexibility is inherent in the value system and kin structure.

In economic concerns the migrants are equally flexible. Rarely does a family's income depend on only one source: far more likely it consists of a combination of strategies which vary according to season and opportunity. Often economic strategies are a function of the flexible social network; that is, a migrant finds a job through or works with a relative or compadre. Social and economic concerns also come together in the system of reciprocal obligation which enables the highlanders to carry out elaborate celebrations such as weddings and saint's day fiestas. Just as they excel at maintaining numerous social alliances, the squatter settlement residents are adept at earning money or trading labor in a variety of ways. Thus the built-in flexibility of the highland kin and alliance systems serves the migrants well in their adaptation to urban life. Despite the sometimes harsh conditions of squatter settlement living the residents retain control over their lives through their energetic and ingenious strategies of coping with hardship and seizing opportunities for living the kind of life they desire.

CONCLUSIONS

This book describes life in Ciudadela Chalaca and Dulanto through the 1970s, focusing on the urbanization process, the adaptation of migrants, and the social organization in these two settlements. The goal is to delineate the basic process of urbanization and to offer some understanding of why urbanization has occurred as it has. I have not tried to predict the results but rather to understand the workings of the system. The following discussion provides an analytical structure through which to view the descriptive material presented in the book.

I began with basically simple but also essential questions regarding how people in the squatter settlements live. What are the goals of the migrants? Why do they choose certain goals? Why do they pursue their goals in the ways that they do? Have the migrants living in the squatter settlements been able to succeed in the process of change to an urban setting? If so, how? And why did they choose the route to an urban life that they did? It is from these questions that the following discussion is derived.

The process of urbanization discussed here is an example of positive adaptation. As with terms such as *poverty,* the concept of positive adaptation must be defined relative to the setting in which it is found. It is evident that life in Ciudadela Chalaca and Dulanto is by no means perfect, nor even easy. The migrants exist in an extremely difficult and at times precarious situation in terms of their access to the resources necessary for survival. Yet from their viewpoint, as described here, they are succeeding. There is no absolute measure of positive or successful adaptation; it changes with time and place and with the people who migrate. Thus, positive adaptation must be defined primarily in the migrants' own terms and measured by their own criteria. There are three criteria for successful or positive adaptation as found in the squatter settlements of Lima.

The first criterion is the ability to build a community both in a material sense and in spirit. Both Ciudadela Chalaca and Dulanto were constructed through the efforts of the people who live there. Although by some standards Ciudadela Chalaca lacks numerous facilities that would make it a model community in a physical sense, the ability of the migrants to build a community to meet their basic needs is impressive. As documented here, life in Ciudadela Chalaca and Dulanto is characterized by active gregariousness in which each individual is the central node in a large network of alliances among kinsmen and paisanos, as well as other forms of alliance. The spirit of community finds its most concentrated expression in the rites of intensification, in which one of the functions is expressing kin, paisano, or community-wide solidarity. The frequency and often the intensity with which these celebrations take place in the squatter settlements is an indication of the continuing reification of the sense of community that exists. A dramatic example of this sense of unity is seen in the group euphoria that often develops during the all-night dancing, drinking, and feasting that accompanies celebrations such as the Fiesta of San Pedro.

The second criterion is the migrants' sense of accomplishing their goals. The most commonly expressed goals of the migrants living in the squatter settlements are obtaining an education for their children, owning their own houses, acquiring appliances, and gaining access to urban amenities. These goals also hold strong symbolic significance in that they imply upward mobility.

Most of the residents of Ciudadela Chalaca and Dulanto view the very act of migration as having conferred upward mobility. In spite of the dense population, the rudimentary sanitation and housing, and the often grueling working conditions and hours in the squatter settlements, the migrants view life there as an improvement over life in the highlands. Thus they see migration itself as an accomplished goal, while other goals, such as education and home ownership, are being attained to differing degrees by each individual.

Goals are attained through a number of strategies. One is the pattern, strongly backed by widely shared values, of working hard and untiringly toward a clearly envisioned and delineated goal. The second strategy is accumulating resources and saving money. This is most strikingly evidenced in the migrants' ability to plan and carry out the extravagant and ostentatious demonstrations of wealth found during such celebrations as wedding and patron saint's fiestas. The third strategy for goal attainment is the maintenance of flexibility through the opening of numerous options and the mobilization of a network of kin and non-kin who will provide aid and support through reciprocal obligations.

The third criterion is the migrants' achievement of a positive view of themselves and their future. Throughout this study, those living in Ciudadela Chalaca and Dulanto are consistently depicted as individually and collectively future-oriented, vigorous people who have a deep sense of confidence in themselves and their ability to effect what they define as positive changes in their lives. This sense of pioneering optimism is even evident among those migrants who have lived in the squatter settlements for twenty years or more.

A number of conditions affect whether positive or negative adaptation accompanies migration from a rural to an urban area. In the two districts that were the focus of this study, four basic conditions determine the process of positive adaptation.

The first condition is the maintenance of core relationships that existed in the premigration rural setting. These core relationships provide a stability that is vital to the physical and emotional well-being of the migrants. Almost all the people who live in Ciudadela Chalaca and Dulanto are surrounded by and daily interact with a vast number of kinsmen and paisanos. The residence pattern, both in Ciudadela Chalaca prior to the remodeling and in both Ciudadela Chalaca and Dulanto after the relocation, is such that population density encourages increased social interaction compared to the often isolated highland villages. Additionally, there is the commonly held value that it is natural and desirable to be in close contact with many people. To be alone is to be unhappy and desolate; one's image of success and happiness is only a reflection of one's position in a large and active social network. The positive value given to being with people facilitates the maintenance of core relationships.

Figure 6.1 presents a series of concentric circles as a model of kin relations. The relationships with people within the circle closest to each person — the family of procreation and his or her siblings — are considered core relationships. The core kinsmen play an important role in the highland setting, and because migrants from the same town tend to live near one another in the city and aid one another in their initial adjustments, there is the clear potential for core kinsmen likewise to play a vital role during the urbanization process. In Ciudadela Chalaca and Dulanto, the family of procreation is the basic economic unit, and it also offers the basic emotional and physical support that is essential during adaptation. The migrants also retain a strong belief in the essential nature of sibling solidarity, which is established early in childhood as elder siblings care for their younger brothers and sisters, creating not only a tie of responsibility but also a sense of interdependency based on birth order. During the initial stages of adaptation, siblings play a paramount role in providing support and aid to newly arrived migrants. Often siblings live near one another and eventually work together in joint commercial enterprises. In addition, the core kinsmen, especially siblings, are vital in carrying out many large-scale events, such as marriage parties and wakes. They also frequently form the basis of membership in voluntary associations, such as soccer teams and electric cooperatives.

The second condition affecting the success of the migrants' adaptation to urban life is the existence of traditional methods of forming alliances that allow an individual to strengthen existing ties and enter into new types of relationships. Structurally, alliances activated by the establishment of reciprocal obligations are an extension of the personal network characteristic of a bilateral kin system. This discussion treats alliances primarily in terms of marriage, *compadrazgo*, economic alliances, and voluntary associations. It places particular emphasis on the marriage tie because of its importance for the migrants in uniting extended families, in adding additional strength to the sibling tie, and in resolving the dilemma of allegiances among an individual's siblings, his or her family of procreation, and affines. In a society in which a large network of alliances is viewed as a treasured resource, the traditional means of forming alliances are extremely useful mechanisms brought from the highlands and exercised in settlements such as Ciudadela Chalaca and Dulanto.

Although all four conditions for successful adaptation are interrelated, the first two conditions especially complement each other, because positive adaptation depends fundamentally on the degree and manner in which it is possible both to maintain stability by maintaining core relationships and to keep open the option for varying relationships by forming alliances.

The third condition is a sense of control over one's own life, that is, a sense of autonomy with respect to forces external to the squatter settlement in making decisions regarding strategies for attaining such goals as the timing of migration or house construction. This sense of control and how it is exercised is discussed here in regard to house construction in both Ciudadela Chalaca and Dulanto, in the choice of economic endeavors and the creation of economic strategies, and in the utilization of both traditional Andean and innovative forms of rites of intensification to fulfill urban needs.

The fourth condition is the existence of a fundamental flexibility in the social structure that underlies all social interaction and that allows for active substitution of forms and functions to suit the urban environment. This characteristic flexibility, which is based on a system of bilateral kindred and a social network activated through balanced reciprocity, is described here in some detail. For example, in the city, where the full complement of core kinsmen may not be present, sibling solidarity may be extended so that first cousins are substituted for siblings and utilized in sibling functions. Or, in the absence of an eldest sibling in the city, the next sibling in age may fulfill the functions normally performed by the eldest. Thus the network of kinsmen based on a bilateral model allows for considerable substitution of roles and functions to suit the different urban environment. This flexibility is based not only on structural characteristics but also on values that give positive connotations to the concepts of change and urbanization.

This study thus identifies four conditions as determinants of the process of positive adaptation in Lima. There is no single cause but rather a shifting cluster of conditions that affect people's modes of adaptation. Urbanization is a continuing, long-term process. Only the initial stages are included in this study: arrival after migration, the establishment of a foothold in the city, and the building of communities and their institutions. It is my hope that the ideas in this book will act as a stimulus to thinking about rural to urban migration by Native People in other parts of the hemisphere, as well as forms of large-scale migration throughout the hemisphere.

BIBLIOGRAPHY

Abu-Lughod, Janet
1961 Migrant Adjustment to City Life: The Egyptian Case. *American Journal of Sociology*, Vol. 67, pp. 22–32.

Adams, Bert N.
1968 *Kinship in an Urban Setting.* Markham Publishing Co., Chicago.

Alberti, Giorgio, and Mayer, Enrique
1974 *Reciprocidad e intercambio en los Andes peruanos.* Instituto de Estudios Peruanos, Problema 12, Lima.

Alers, Oscar, and Applebaum, Richard P.
1968 La migración en el Perú: un invertario de proposiciones. *Centro de Estudios de Población y Desarrollo*, Vol. 1, No. 4, Lima.

Anderson, Nels
1959 Urbanism and Urbanization. *American Journal of Sociology*, Vol. 65, No. 1, pp. 68–73.

Area de Salud de Callao
1964 *Estudio de las barriadas de Callao.* Lima.

Arensberg, Conrad M.
1968 The Urban in Crosscultural Perspective. In *Urban Anthropology Research Perspectives and Strategies,* edited by Elizabeth M. Eddy. *Southern Anthropological Society Proceedings,* No. 2, Athens, Georgia.

Arguedas, José María
1952 El complejo cultural en el Perú y el primer congreso de peruanistas. *América indígena,* Vol. 2, No. 2, pp. 131–139.

Ashton, Guy T.
1972 The Differential Adaptation of Two Slum Subcultures to a Colombian Housing Project. *Urban Anthropology,* Vol. 1, No. 2, pp. 176–194.

Banton, Michael
1966 *The Social Anthropology of Complex Societies.* Oxford University Press, London.

Berckholtz, P.
1963 *Barrios marginales, aberración social.* Lima.

Bolton, Ralph
1977 The Qolla marriage process. In *Andean Kinship and Marriage,* edited by Ralph Bolton and Enrique Mayer. Special publication of the American Anthropology Association, No. 7, Washington, D.C.

Bolton, Ralph, and Mayer, Enrique, eds.
1977 *Andean Kinship and Marriage.* Special publication of the American Anthropology Association, No. 7, Washington, D.C.

Browning, Harley L.
1958 Recent Trends in Latin American Urbanization. *Annals of the American Academy of Political and Social Sciences,* Vol. 318, pp. 111–120. Philadelphia.
1972 Primacy Variation in Latin America During the Twentieth Century. In *XXXIX Congreso Internacional de Americanistas,* Lima.

Brush, Stephen B.
1974 Peru's Invisible Migrants. Paper presented to 1974 Annual Meeting, American Anthropological Association, Mexico City.
1977 Kinship and Land Use in a Northern Sierra Community. In *Andean Kinship and Marriage,* edited by Ralph Bolton and Enrique Mayer. Special publication of the American Anthropology Association, No. 7, Washington, D.C.

Bryce-LaPorte, Roy S.
1968 Family Adaptation of Relocated Slum Dwellers in Puerto Rico: Implications for Urban Research and Development. *Journal of Developing Areas,* Vol. 2, pp. 533–540.

Butterworth, C.
1962 A Study of the Urbanization Process Among Mixtec Migrants From Tilantongo in Mexico City. *América indígena*, Vol. 22, pp. 257–274.

Cancian, Frank
1965 *Economics and Prestige in a Naya Community.* Stanford University Press.

Carter, William E.
1977 Trial Marriage in the Andes? (Irpa Chico, an Aymara Community in Bolivia). In *Andean Kinship and Marriage*, edited by Ralph Bolton and Enrique Mayer. Special publication of the American Anthrolopogy Association, No. 7, Washington, D.C.

Colter, Julio
1959 *Los cambios en la propiedad, la comunidad y la familia en San Lorenzo de Quinti.* Instituto de Etnología y Arqueología, Lima.

Custred, Glynn
1977 Peasant Kinship, Subsistence and Economics in a High Altitude Andean Environment. In *Andean Kinship and Marriage*, edited by Ralph Bolton and Enrique Mayer. Special publication of the American Anthropology Association, No. 7, Washington, D.C.

DeGregori, Carlos, and Golte, Jurgen
1973 *Dependencia y desintegración estructural en la comunidad de Pacaraos.* Instituto de Estudios Peruanos, Lima.

Delgado, Carlos
1968 *Tres planteamientos en torno a problemas de urbanización acelerada en areas metropolitanas: El caso de Lima.* Cuadernos Plandemet, Lima.
1969 An Analysis of Arribismo in Peru. *Human Organization*, Vol. 28, No. 2, pp. 133–139.

Dirección Nacional de Estadística y Censos
1968 *Encuesta de inmigración de Lima metropolitana, tercer informe.* Lima.

Doughty, Paul
1965 The Interrelationship of Power, Respect, Affection and Rectitude in Vicos. *Behavioral Science*, Vol. 8, No. 7, p. 3.
1970 Behind the Back of the City: Provincial Life in Lima, Peru. In *Peasants in Cities: Readings in the Anthropology of Urbanization*, edited by W. Mangin. Houghton Mifflin Company, Boston.

Epstein, A. L.
1967 Urbanization and Social Change in Africa. *Current Anthropology*, Vol. 8, No. 4, pp. 275–296.

Escobar, Gabriel
1973 *Sicaya: cambios culturales en una comunidad mestiza andina.* Instituto de Estudios Peruanos, Lima.

Faron, Louis C.
1960 The Formation of Two Indigenous Communities in Coastal Peru. *American Anthropologist,* Vol. 62, pp. 437–453.

Foster, George M.
1953 Cofradía and Compadrazgo in Spain and Spanish America. *Southwest Journal of Anthropology,* No. 9, pp. 1–28.
1965 Peasant Society and the Image of Limited Good. *American Anthropologist,* Vol. 67, pp. 293–315.
1972 A Second Look at Limited Good. *Anthropological Quarterly,* Vol. 45, pp. 57–64.

Fox, Robin
1967 *Kinship and Marriage: An Anthropological Perspective.* Penguin Books, Harmondsworth.

Fried, Jacob
1959 Acculturation and Mental Health Among Indian Migrants in Peru. In *Culture and Mental Health,* edited by M. K. Opler. The Macmillan Company, New York.

Fuenzalida, Fernando
1970 Poder, raza, y etnia en el Perú contemporaneo. In *El indio y el poder,* edited by José Matos Mar. Instituto Estudios Peruanos, Lima.

Fuenzalida, Fernando; Villarán, José Luis; Golte, Jurgen; Valiente, Teresa
1968 *Estructural tradicional y economía de mercado: la comunidad de indígenas de Huayopampa.* Instituto de Estudios Peruanos, Lima.

Gans, Herbert J.
1962 *The Urban Villagers: Group and Class in the Life of Italian-Americans.* Free Press, New York.

Gillin, John
1945 *Moche: A Peruvian Coastal Community.* Smithsonian Institution, Washington, D.C.

Goodenough, Ward
1970 *Description and Comparison in Cultural Anthropology.* Aldine Publishing Company, Chicago.

Graburn, Nelson
1971 *Readings in Kinship and Social Structure.* Harper and Row, New York.

Hammel, Eugene A.
1965 Review of the Ceque System of Cuzco. *American Anthropologist,* Vol. 67, pp. 780–785.

1969 *Power in Ica: The Structural History of a Peruvian Community.* Little, Brown and Company, Boston.

Heath, Dwight (Ed.)
1974 *Contemporary Cultures and Societies of Latin America.* Random House, New York.

Isbell, Billie Jean
1973 Andean Structures and Activities: Towards a Study of Transformations of Traditional Concepts in a Central Highland Peasant Community. Doctoral dissertation, University of Illinois, Urbana.
1974 The Essential Other Half: A Study of Andean Sexual Complementarity. Unpublished manuscript.
1977 "Those Who Love Me," An Analysis of Andean Kinship and Reciprocity Within a Ritual Context. In *Andean Kinship and Marriage,* edited by Ralph Bolton and Enrique Mayer. Special publication of the American Anthropology Association, No. 7, Washington, D.C.

Keesing, Roger M.
1966 Kwaio Kindreds. *Southwestern Journal of Anthropology,* Vol. 22, p. 346.

Kemper, Robert V.
1970 The Anthropological Study of Migration to Latin American Cities. *Kroeber Anthropological Society Papers,* No. 42, pp. 1–25. Berkeley.
1974*a* Family and Household Organization Among Tzintzuntzan Migrants in Mexico City. In *Latin American Urban Research,* Vol. 4, edited by Wayne Cornelius and Felicity Trueblood. Sage Publications, Beverly Hills.
1974*b* Tzintzuneños in Mexico City: The Anthropologist Among Peasant Migrants. In *Anthropologists in Cities,* edited by George M. Foster and Robert V. Kemper. Little, Brown and Company, Boston.

Kemper, Robert V., and Foster, George M.
1975 Urbanization in Mexico: The View from Tzintzuntzan. In *Urbanization and Inequality: The Political Economy of Urban and Rural Development in Latin America,* edited by Wayne Cornelius and Felicity Trueblood. Sage Publications, Beverly Hills.

LaLone, Darrell E.
1971 Cholification and the Nationalization of Peruvian Society: A Crisis in Peruvian National Development. *California Anthropologist,* Vol. 1, No. 2, pp. 1–17.

Lambert, Bernard
1977 Bilaterality in the Andes. In *Andean Kinship and Marriage,* edited by Ralph Bolton and Enrique Mayer. Special publication of the American Anthropology Association, No. 7, Washington, D.C.

Lewis, Oscar
1952 Urbanization Without Breakdown. *Scientific Monthly*, Vol. 75, No. 1, pp. 31–41.
1962 *Five Families: Mexican Case Studies in the Culture of Poverty*. John Wiley & Sons, New York.
1966 The Culture of Poverty. *Scientific American*, Vol. 215, No. 4, pp. 19–25.

Ley de las Barriadas
1961 Editorial Thesis, Law 13517. Lima.

Liebow, Elliot
1967 *Tally's Corner*. Little, Brown and Company, Boston.

Lloyd, Peter C.
1975 The World View of a Shanty Town Population. Paper presented to the First Peruvian Psychology Congress, Lima.

Lobo, Frank
1970 An Example of Indigenous Community Development in a Peruvian Squatter Settlement. Unpublished manuscript, Department of Anthropology, University of Arizona, Tucson.

Lomnitz, Larissa
1974 The Social and Economic Organization of a Mexican Shantytown. In *Latin American Urban Research*, edited by Wayne Cornelius and Felicity Trueblood. Sage Publications, Beverly Hills.
1977 *Networks and Marginality: Life in a Mexican Shantytown*. Academic Press, Inc., New York.

MacEwen, Alison M.
1973 Kinship and Mobility on the Argentine Pampa. *Ethnology*, Vol. 12, No. 2, pp. 135–151.

Mangin, William
1955a The Role of Regional Associations in the Adaptation of Rural Population in Peru. *Sociologus*, Vol. 9, pp. 21–36. Berlin.
1960 Mental Health and Migration to Cities. *Annals of the New York Academy of Sciences*, Vol. 84, No. 17, pp. 911–917.
1967a Latin American Squatter Settlements: A Problem and a Solution. *Latin American Research Review*, Vol. 2, No. 3, pp. 65–90.
1967b Las comunidades alteñas en la América Latina. *Serie de antropología social*, 5. Instituto Indígena Interamericano, Mexico, D.F.
1970 Similarities and Differences Between Two Types of Peruvian Communities. In *Peasants in Cities: Readings in the Anthropology of Urbanization*, edited by W. Mangin. Houghton Mifflin Company, Boston.
1973 Sociological, Cultural, and Political Characteristics of Some Urban Migrants in Peru. In *Urban Anthropology: Crosscultural Studies of Urbanization*, edited by Aidan Southall. Oxford University Press, New York.

Mangin, W. (Ed.)
1970 *Peasants in Cities: Readings in the Anthropology of Urbanization.* Houghton Mifflin Company, Boston.

Martínez, Hector
1968 Las migraciones internas en el Perú. *Estudios de población y desarrollo,* Vol. 2, No. 1, Lima.

Matos Mar, José
1964*a* El campesino costeño. In *Cuadernos de antropología.* Universidad Nacional Mayor de San Marcos, Vol. 2, No. 2, pp. 1–12.
1964*b* La propiedad en la isla de Taquile. In *Estudios sobre la cultura actual del Perú.* Universidad Nacional Mayor de San Marcos, Lima.
1966*a* La urbanización y los cambios en la sociedad y cultura peruana. *Cuadernos de antropología,* Vol. IV, No. 9, pp. 1–10.
1966*b* *Estudio de las barriadas limeñas.* Departamento de Antropologia, Lima.
1968 *Urbanización y barriadas en América del Sur.* Instituto de Estudios Peruanos, Lima.

Mayer, Enrique
1977 Beyond the Nuclear Family. In *Andean Kinship and Marriage,* edited by Ralph Bolton and Enrique Mayer. Special publication of the American Anthropology Association, No. 7, Washington, D.C.

Mejía Valera, José
1966 Desorganización social. Unpublished manuscript, Lima.

Millones, Luis
1975 *La cultura colonial urbana: una hipótesis del trabajo para el estudio de las poblaciones tugurizadas.* Pontificia Universidad Católica del Perú. Lima.

Ministerio de Salud Público y Asistencia Social
1961 *Barriadas de Lima Metropolitana.* Lima.

Mintz, Sidney, and Wolf, Eric
1950 An Analysis of Ritual Co-parenthood. *Southwest Journal of Anthropology,* Vol. 6, pp. 341–368.

Morris, Earl W.; Brownrigg, Leslie; Bourque, Susan; and Dobyns, Henry
1968 *Coming Down the Mountain: The Social Worlds of Mayobamba.* Andean Indian Community Research and Development Program, Department of Anthropology, Cornell University, Ithaca.

Murdock, George
1949 *Social Structure.* The Macmillan Company, New York.

Murra, John V.
1962 Cloth and Its Functions in the Inca State. *American Anthropologist,* Vol. 64, No. 4, pp. 710–728.

Oficina Nacional de Estadística y Censos
1969 *Informe de la encuesta de fecundidad en el Agustino*, Lima.
1972 Los pueblos jovenes en el Perú. *Boletín de análisis demográfico*, Vol. 13. Lima.
1974a *Censos nacionales VII de población, II de vivienda del Departamento de Lima*. Talleres de la Imprenta del Ministerio de Guerra, Lima.
1947b Perú: crecimiento demográfico y desarrollo económico y social; repuesta a la segunda encuesta de los Naciones Unidas. Lima.
1974c *Censos nacionales VII de población, II de vivienda*. Provincial Constitucional del Callao, Talleres de la Imprenta del Ministerio de Guerra, Lima.
1974d Indices de los precios al consumidor, Lima.

Orlove, Benjamin
1974 Reciprocipad, desigualdad y dominación. In *Reciprocidad e intercambio en los Andes peruanos*, edited by Giorgio Alberti and Enrique Mayer. Instituto de Estudios Peruanos, Lima.

Paredes, Ernesto
1963 Fuentes de la población de la barriada Fray Martín de Porres. In *Migración e integración en el Perú*, edited by Henry Dobyns and Mario Vázquez. *Monografías andinas*, No. 2. Lima.

Patch, Richard W.
1957 Life in a Callejón: A Study of Urban Disorganization. *American Universities Field Staff, West Coast South America Series*, Vol. 1, No. 6, Lima.
1959 How Communal are the Communities? *American Universities Field Staff, Latin America*, Vol. 6, No. 5, Lima.
1967 La Parada, Lima's Market: Part I, A Villager Who Met Disaster; Part II, Serrano and Criollo: The Confusion of Race With Class; Part III, Serrano to Criollo: A Study of Assimilation. *American Universities Field Staff, West Coast South America Series*, Vol. 14, No. 3. Peru.

Peattie, Lisa Redfield
1970 *The View From the Barrio*. University of Michigan Press, Ann Arbor.

Perlman, Janice
1973 Río's Favelados and the Myth of Marginality. *Institute of Urban and Regional Development*, Working Paper No. 222. University of California, Berkeley.

Plotnicov, Leonard
1973 Anthropological Field Work in Modern and Local Urban Contexts. *Urban Anthropology*, Vol. 2, No. 2, pp. 248–264.

Radcliffe-Brown, A. R., and Forde, Daryll (Eds.)
1950 *African Systems of Kinship and Marriage*. Oxford University Press, London.

Reategui, Ulises
1971 *Invasores?* Ediciones Barriales, Lima.

Rowe, John H.
1947 The Incas. In *Handbook of South American Indians,* edited by Julian
Steward, Vol. 2. U.S. Government Printing Office, Washington, D.C.

Safa, Helen Icken
1974 *The Urban Poor of Puerto Rico: A Study in Development and Inequality.* Holt, Rinehart and Winston, Inc., New York.

Smith, T. Lynn
1964 Urbanization in Latin America. In *Urbanism and Urbanization,*
edited by Nels Anderson, pp. 127–142. E. J. Brill, Leiden.

Spicer, Edward H.
1940 *Pascua: A Yaqui Village in Arizona.* University of Chicago Press,
Chicago.

Stack, Carol B.
1972 Black Kindreds: Parenthood and Personal Kindreds Among Urban
Blacks. *Journal of Comparative Family Studies,* Vol. 1, No. 1, pp.
195–203.

Stein, William H.
1961 *Hualcán: Life in the Highlands of Peru.* Cornell University Press,
Ithaca.

Steward, Julian, and Faron, Louis
1959 *Native Peoples of South America.* McGraw-Hill, New York.

Stycos, Joseph, and Dobyns, Cara Richards de
1963 Fuentes de la migración en la gran Lima. In *Migración e integración en el Perú,* edited by Henry Dobyns and Mario Vásquez. *Monografías andinas,* No. 2, Lima.

Suttles, Gerald
1968 *The Social Order of the Slum.* University of Chicago Press, Chicago.

Torero, Alfredo
1972 Lingüística e historia de la sociedad andina. In *El reto del multi-
lingüismo en el Perú,* edited by Alberto Escobar. Instituto de Estudios
Peruanos, Lima.

Turner, John C.
1965 Lima's Barriadas and Corralones: Suburbs Versus Slums. *Ekistics,*
No. 112, March.
1967 Barriers and Channels for Housing Development in Modernizing
Counties. *American Institute of Planners Journal,* pp. 167–182.

Uzzell, John Douglas
1972 Bound for Places I'm Not Known To: Adaptation of Migrants and Residence in Four Irregular Settlements in Lima, Peru. Doctoral dissertation, University of Texas at Austin.

Valdivia, Oscar
1970 *Migración interna a la metrópoli: contraste cultural, conflicto y desadaptación.* Universidad Nacional Mayor de San Marcos, Lima.

Varallanos, José
1962 *El cholo y el Perú. Introducción al estudio sociológico de un hombre y un pueblo mestizo y su destino cultural.* Imprenta López, Buenos Aires.

Vásquez, Mario, and Holmberg, Allan
1966 The Castas: Unilineal Kin Groups in Vicos, Peru. *Ethnology*, Vol. 5, pp. 284–303.

Weaver, Thomas, and White, Douglas
1972 Anthropological Approaches to Urban and Complex Society. In *The Anthropology of Urban Environments*, edited by Thomas Weaver and Douglas White. The Society for Applied Anthropology Monograph Series 11.

Webster, Steven S.
1977 Kinship and Affinity in a Native Quechua Community. In *Andean Kinship and Marriage*, edited by Ralph Bolton and Enrique Mayer. Special publication of the American Anthropology Association, No. 7, Washington, D.C.

Whyte, William F.
1969 Consideraciones generales de una teoría de los procesos socialies. In *Dominación y cambios en el Perú rural*, edited by José Matos. Instituto de Estudios Peruanos, Lima.

Young, Michael, and Willmott, Peter
1957 *Family and Kinship in East London.* Routledge and Kegan Paul, Ltd., London.

Zuidema, R. T.
1964 *The Ceque System of Cuzco: The Social Organization of the Capital of the Inca.* E. J. Brill, Leiden.

INDEX

Note: The following index is reproduced from the original edition and does not include references to the text of either the new preface or the new conclusion.